CHRISTMAS COMIC Posters

HOORAY FOR FATHER CHRISTMAS.

A JOLLY XMAS

A Denis Gifford Collection

CHRISTMAS COMIC Posters

A Denis Gifford Collection

BLOSSOM

An H.C. Blossom Book

Copyright © text and compilation Denis Gifford 1991

Copyright © Comics: as listed opposite

ISBN 1 872532 57 8

Design: Roger Lightfoot

Typeset in Great Britain by Uppercase

Printed and bound in Hong Kong

H.C. Blossom
6/7 Warren Mews
London W1P 5DJ

Copyright Acknowledgements
These comics all come from the author's collection. The original publishers are acknowledged herewith.

Ally Sloper's Half-Holiday © 16 December 1884; December 1922 The Sloperies
Beano Comic © 14 December 1940 D.C. Thomson Ltd
Big Budget © 10 December 1904 C. Arthur Pearson Ltd
Bo-Peep © 24 December 1932 Amalgamated Press Ltd
Boys and Girls Daily Mail © 22 December 1934 Associated Press Ltd
Bubbles © 26 December 1925 Amalgamated Press Ltd
Chicks' Own © 18 December 1926 Amalgamated Press Ltd
Chips © 27 December 1941 Amalgamated Press Ltd
Christmas Comic © 24 November 1933 C. Arthur Pearson Ltd
Chuckles © 25 November 1916 Amalgamated Press Ltd
Comic Cuts © 4 December 1897 Harmsworth Brothers
Comic Life © 17 December 1910 James Henderson Ltd
Comic News © 21 December 1863 Maddick & Pottage
Crackers © 30 December 1933 Amalgamated Press Ltd
Dandy Comic © 14 December 1940 D.C. Thomson Ltd
Everyday Novels and Comics © December 1940 Popular Fiction
Funny Folks © December 1877 James Henderson Ltd
Funny Wonder © 19 December 1896 Harmsworth Brothers
Golden Fun and Story © 25 December 1937 Amalgamated Press Ltd
Happy Days © 24 December 1938 Amalgamated Press Ltd
Jingles © 28 December 1935 Amalgamated Press Ltd
Joker © 2 January 1937 Amalgamated Press Ltd
Jolly Jack's Weekly © 24 December 1933 Associated Press Ltd
Jolly Jumbo's Christmas Comic © 16 November 1936 C. Arthur Pearson Ltd
Jungle Jinks © 13 December 1934 Amalgamated Press Ltd
Knockout Comic and Magnet © 28 December 1940 Amalgamated Press Ltd
Larks © 19 December 1898 Trapps, Holmes & Co
Lot o' Fun © 25 December 1909 James Henderson Ltd
Magic Comic © 14 December 1940 D.C. Thomson Ltd
Merry and Bright © 23 December 1933 Amalgamated Press Ltd
Merry Moments © 20 December 1919 George Newnes Ltd
Mickey Mouse Weekly © 26 December 1936 Odhams/Willbank/Walt Disney
My Favourite Comic © 26 December 1931 Amalgamated Press Ltd
Playbox © 24 December 1938 Amalgamated Press Ltd
Playtime © 22 December 1928 Amalgamated Press Ltd
Puck © 15 December 1906; 26 December 1937 Amalgamated Press Ltd
Radio Fun © 24 December 1938 Amalgamated Press Ltd
Rainbow © 15 December 1917 Amalgamated Press Ltd
Sparkler © 28 December 1935 Amalgamated Press Ltd
Sunbeam © 2 January 1932 Amalgamated Press Ltd
Tiger Tim's Weekly © 27 December 1924 Amalgamated Press Ltd
Tiny Tots © 19 December 1936 Amalgamated Press Ltd
Tip Top © 28 December 1935 Amalgamated Press Ltd
Xmas Holiday Comic © 22 November 1936 C. Arthur Pearson Ltd

Contents

Introduction

Have a Comic Christmas, Chums!

When icicles hang by the wall,
And Barney Boko blows his nose,
Then nightly sing the Casey Court Carollers!
Tu-whit, tu-whoo, a merry note,
While Keyhole Kate doth keel her pote!

Pardon my garbled bard, folks, but the impending Yuletide brings me out in early snow-balls, a symptom suffered by us old pros in the comic game – and indeed in all walks of professional publishing – for ways to enhance a reader's Happy Christmas need to be dreamed up some time in advance. Thus while I type this amid a season of mists and mellow fruitfulness, you will be reading it in the thick of seasonal snow and mistletoe. At least if our comic artists have anything to do with it, you will. For while our well-loved weather tends more and more to slip out of natural synchronisation, so that we have sunshine in Winter and snow in Summer, the traditions of comic publishing remain rooted in that legacy of long-lost yule-loggery bequeathed to us by Charles Dickens and Co. And who would have it any other way? For Christmas time is when children's comics come into their own, generously ladling the lettering with dollops of snow, decorating the panels with streamers round the borders and mistletoe in the corners, and serving up steaming cannon-balls of plum puddings, dripping with custard and decked with holly, for last-picture parties.

Were our childhood Christmasses really like that, or are our aging memories braised with second-hand slap-ups from our comics? A bit of both, perhaps, to be kind to our Mums and Dads; but never-oh-never was there such jubilant jollification among the jellies as penned by the pre-war comic artists of England. And never-oh-never was any Christmas comic as Christ-massy as the Christmas number of *Happy Days!* This was the finest feather in the party hat of the old Amalgamated Press, foremost publisher of juvenile entertainment on paper since Alfred Harmsworth founded it in the 1890s. *Happy Days* was their first full-colour comic to be printed in photogravure, created to compete with their arch rival, Odhams Press, who were proud publishers of Walt Disney's wonderment, *Mickey Mouse Weekly*.

Happy Days, a big, bold tabloid of twelve pages for twopence, was launched on an unsuspecting young world on 8 October 1938. The cover alone was worth the entrance fee. *At Chimpo's Circus* (actually the title formed part of the comic's title, so the strip was really called *Happy Days at Chimpo's Circus*), was a riot of funny animals as only Roy Wilson could draw them. And here was another departure for the Amalgamated Press. The editor, John L. Bott, was so delighted with Wilson's outstanding artwork that he actually allowed him to sign his name! True, only 'Wilson' was permitted; fans learned of the 'Roy' part much later after this King of Comic Artists left us – tragically never to know how much he was loved by his young readers and worshipped by his peers.

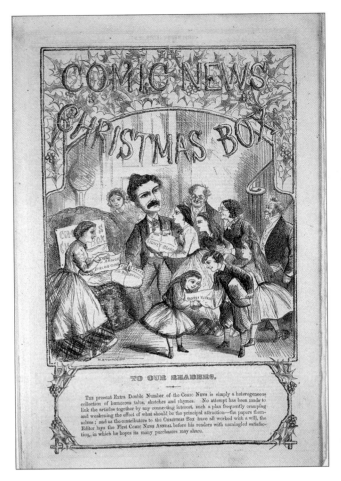

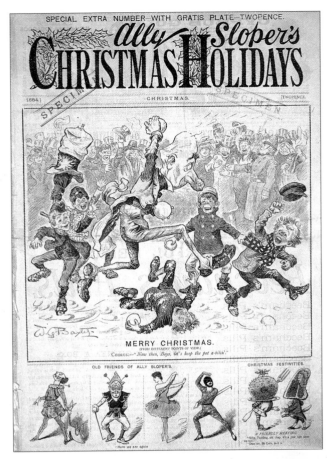

The first Christmas number of the first British comic, drawn by W. McConnell and published on 21 December 1886 by Maddick and Pottage.

The first special Christmas number of the famous comic weekly, Ally Sloper's Half-Holiday, *drawn by William Baxter and published on 16 December 1884 by W. J. Sinkins.*

Royston Warner Wilson had been a fairly successful commercial artist, a graduate of Norwich Art school, when at the age of twenty, in 1920, he had a chance encounter with another, older, and more successful cartoonist in a local pub. This was Donald Newhouse, who had started drawing for children's comics before the Great War, and he took young Wilson on as his assistant. Working as a team, with Newhouse making sure that he did all the lettering, that unfailing means of artist identification in those anonymous days, the combined cartoonists doubled their weekly output, much to the delight of the Amalgamated Press editors, who were equally amazed at the sharp increase in the quality as well as the quantity of black-and-white artwork coming down the line from Norwich.

Wilson and Newhouse not only produced some of the funniest slapstick strips of their day, (*Pitch and Toss* in *Funny Wonder*; *Basil and Bert* in *Jester*), they also drew delightful animal series for the nursery comics – *Pickles the Puppy*, *Bunny the Rabbit*, and even one called *Mickey the Mouse* in *Bubbles*. As a small boy, one of my personal favourites was *The Joyland Express*, which starred two little pigs in pierrot costumes. This strip chugged right across the centre spread of *Sunbeam*, each picture of the story forming a railway carriage being pulled along by a puffy little engine.

By the Thirties the wonder of Wilson had been discovered. Leonard Stroud, the editor of *Butterfly*, exposed Newhouse's secret and made it his business to persuade Wilson to break from his boss and go it alone. So *Steve and Stumpy the World's Worst Cowboys* galloped from Wilson's nib all over the back page of *Butterfly* (Starting at no 714, 13 December 1930) and Wilson was away. Soon every new comic that came from the famous Fleetway House, Farringdon Street, just had to have a Wilson front page. *Jingles* began with *The Tiddlewink Family*, *Jolly* with *Jack Sprat and Tubby Tadpole*, *Radio Fun* with *George the Jolly Gee-Gee*, and, of course, Chimpo in *Happy Days*. Plus an ever-increasing quota of inside strips, of course.

Wilson's comic career continued until his death in the Sixties, but clever as his latterday adventures of Eric Morecambe and Ernie Wise undoubtedly are, it is the pre-war Wilson that we all love, and whose style sums up everything that is unique about British comic art. And never more so than at Christmas. Wilson loved to let himself go on the special occasions that comics loved to celebrate. His fireworks fronts are fun, his celebration specials are stunning, but his Christmas covers are masterworks. And none was so masterly as his *Happy Days Christmas Number:* number thirteen of the comic, as it happened, but never was a superstition more soundly trounced. In fact, there was so much Christmas in Wilson's inkwell that year, that it spilled all over next week's issue, too!

The Christmas *Happy Days* is more than a 'mere' comic, however. It was, as fate would have it, the last truly great Christmas cover ever. For there would never be another Christmas number for *Happy Days*. The comic was discontinued on 5 August 1939, at issue number forty-five. And there would never be another piping pre-war Christmas comic of any kind, because, of course, within a month of *Happy Days'* disappearance, Great Britain would be at war. By December 1939, paper suppliers were already feeling the pinch, noticeably as to the quality of the newsprint itself. Comic artists were already serving in the armed forces, and even after the war, there would be long years of austerity before the New Elizabethan Age of the Fifties allowed new comics to be published in a style that echoed but never truly emulated the Golden Age glory of the Thirties.

This collection stands as a salute to those sumptuous, slapstick days of snowbound, holly-laden Double Numbers which, never priced higher than twopence a copy, might even conceal not one, not two, but *three* grand free gifts for Christmas!

And it is, of course, dedicated to the ever bright memory of Roy Wilson, King of the Comics.

DENIS GIFFORD

FUNNY FOLKS

1887

CHRISTMAS NUMBER.

TWENTY PAGES. **PRICE TWOPENCE.**

MR. JOHN BULLIWIG'S BALL.

Funny Folks Christmas Number

December 1887
James Henderson and Sons

Artist: John Phillips Stafford

Funny Folks, until recently thought to be the first British comic, was subtitled *A Weekly Budget of Funny Pictures, Funny Notes, Funny Jokes, Funny Stories.* It started as an eight-page pull-out supplement to the Christmas Number of *The Weekly Budget* on 12 December 1874, but it was some time before full colour printing could be managed. The cover of this, the first Christmas Extra Number to be printed in colours, was drawn by J. P. Stafford, the weekly's leading cartoonist, who based his idea on a well-known illustration by John Leech out of Charles Dickens.

The Funny Wonder. 1d.

No. 203. Vol. VIII.]   [DECEMBER 19, 1896.

MOWER TROUBLE.

1. It was really Maria's fault. She'd no business to put that skin rug among the long grass when she'd been shaking it.

2. Though, nevertheless, Thomas ought to have noticed it when he came to mow that grass. However, he didn't, and so the rug got mowed too.

3. Of course, to all intents and purposes, the rug was spoilt!!

AT THE KICKTON FOOTBALL MATCH.

1. "Well done our side; a goal certain!"

2. "Missed! by Jupiter!!"

WHY?

Why does little Willie's face wear such a worried look?
(See page 2 for the rest of Little Willie, which explains everything.)

THE REASON.

P.C. HIGGINBOTHAM: "I tell yer, matey, the murderer parsed close to me. I reekernized 'im in a minute."

P.C. BROWNEENOBB: "Then, why in thunder didn't yer h'arrest 'im?"

P.C. HIGGINBOTHAM: "Nas, 'ow could I, with a hummuzzled dawg in one 'and and a whiskey flarsk in the hother. That's wot I don't like about you—you speaks without thinkin'."

A REGULAR TAR-TAR.

1. This is Jorgee Joodle. He is reclining pleasantly against the boat. Alas! he knoweth not that the tar on that boat is still wet.

2. But as the tide came in, and he desired to remove himself, Jorgee found that he had formed a strong attachment for that boat.

3. On came the tide. "Oh! if this tar would only release me, I might yet be saved," moaned Jorgee.

4. (Half an hour later): "Oh! if this tar will only hold me fast I may yet be saved."—Swishy-swish!! Poor Jorgee!

The Funny Wonder Grand Christmas Number

19 December 1896
Messrs Harmsworth

Artists: Frank Holland and others

Alfred Harmsworth and his brothers created the first great boom in British comics with their introduction of *Comic Cuts* on 17 May 1890. *Illustrated Chips* (26 July 1890) and then *The Funny Wonder* (4 February 1893) followed, all sharing the Harmsworth touch, which meant the usual penny price of comics being cut to one halfpenny. Except at Christmas, when full colour printing was introduced by the London Colour Printing Company, causing the cost to be raised to one penny for the special edition.

Double Christmas Number·

Comic Cuts 1ᵈ

No. 395. Vol. XVI.] ONE HALFPENNY WEEKLY. [Dec. 4, 1897.

An extract from "Dungeon Deep," *the new story inside:* "'Your Eminence, I implore you, in the name of heaven, to have mercy! At least, give me time to prepare!' The Cardinal, who had made a movement as if to withdraw, stopped, and turned again to his victim. For fully a minute he stood silently watching him. 'There is but one way to save your life,' he said at last."—*From our new historical novel of the days of Cardinal Wolse and Bluff King Hal and his six wives, beginning in this number.*

ADVENTURES OF CHOKEE BILL, BURGLAR AND AREA SNEAKER.
(Every Week.)

"Dungeon Deep"
(NEW STORY)
Commences To-day.

(1). DEAR MR. EDDITTER.—It was erbout Xmastime, an' I wos burglin' a 'ouse. I bounced in the winder rawther careless.

(2). Just as I'd landed in, I 'ears a shriek, an' sees a lidy wot wos, dowtless, the cook, asittin' there. "Great Pip," I thort, "I'm done for! She'll yell an' wake up the whole show!" Suddenly I gits an idea.

(Continued on page 2.)

Comic Cuts Double Christmas Number

4 December 1897 (no 395)
Messrs Harmsworth

Artists: Frank Holland and others

The first full colour Christmas Number of *Comic Cuts*, Alfred Harmsworth's pioneering halfpenny comic first published on 17 May 1890. Printed by the London Colour Printing Company at their works, Exmoor Street, North Kensington, West London, this sixteen-page edition cost twice the usual price, one penny. *The Adventures of Chokee Bill and Area Sneaker*, a couple of bold, bad burglars, were the current front page heroes, drawn by Frank Holland. This week they had to share the cover with the dramatic illustration to the new serial, *Dungeon Deep*, artist unknown.

Christmas Larks!

TUPMAN, WINKLE, AND SNODGRASS, AND THE CHRISTMAS LEGEND OF CASTLE MANOR.

1.—"THE legend runs thus," said the Host of Castle Manor, to his assembled guests on Xmas Eve. "During the Civil War, three of my ancestors were murdered by eating poisoned Xmas pudding one Xmas Eve. Their three spirits, clad in sombre garments, and carrying a huge Xmas pudding, wander slowly every festive season through the corridors of this mansion."

4.—Now, most of the guests were just about to retire to their respective rooms, when the ghostly trio suddenly appeared on the scene. "The spirits! the three murdered ancestors!!" they screamed, and a general stampede took place.

2.—Now Tup., Wink., and Snod. (who had been engaged for Xmas week as waiters), overheard this legend, and late that night, might have been seen packing up gold and silver plate, jewellery, &c., in a huge, dark, spotty cloth.

5.—In the midst of the confusion, Tup., Wink., and Snod. (for it was our three friends), got clear away from the castle, and, throwing aside their disguises, tore off with the booty, which they had so ingeniously packed to resemble the pudding.

3.—And at about 1 A.M., three weird-looking objects, clad in flowing garments, and carrying a huge Xmas pudding (?) started slowly and solemnly forth to patrol the corridors of the ancient castle.

6.—The scene changes. We are again in the humble lodgings of the merry trio. Winkle is proposing a toast—"Success to the Legend of Castle Manor, and a Merry Christmas and Happy New Year to the readers of LARKS!" And so say all of us.

Christmas Larks!

19 December 1898 (no 295)
Trapps, Holmes and Co

Artist: Will Spurrier

The first full colour Christmas Number of *Larks!*, a halfpenny comic begun by Gilbert Dalziell, the publisher of *Ally Sloper's Half-Holiday* on 1 May 1893. The comic was taken over by cheapo publishers Trapps, Homes and Co from 9 December 1895. This issue was specially printed in colours by Harrison and Sons of St Martin's Lane, and provided a bumper twenty-page comic for one penny. *Tupman*, *Winkle* and *Snodgrass*, names redolent of Charles Dickens, were drawn by Will Spurrier, the comic's leading artist.

THE GORGEOUS DOUBLE XMAS

BigBudget 2D

EDITOR: ARTHUR BROOKE.

Week ending Dec. 10, 1904.
Vol. XVI. No. 391. Price 2d.

ART EDITOR: YORICK

Wishing You A Merry Christmas!

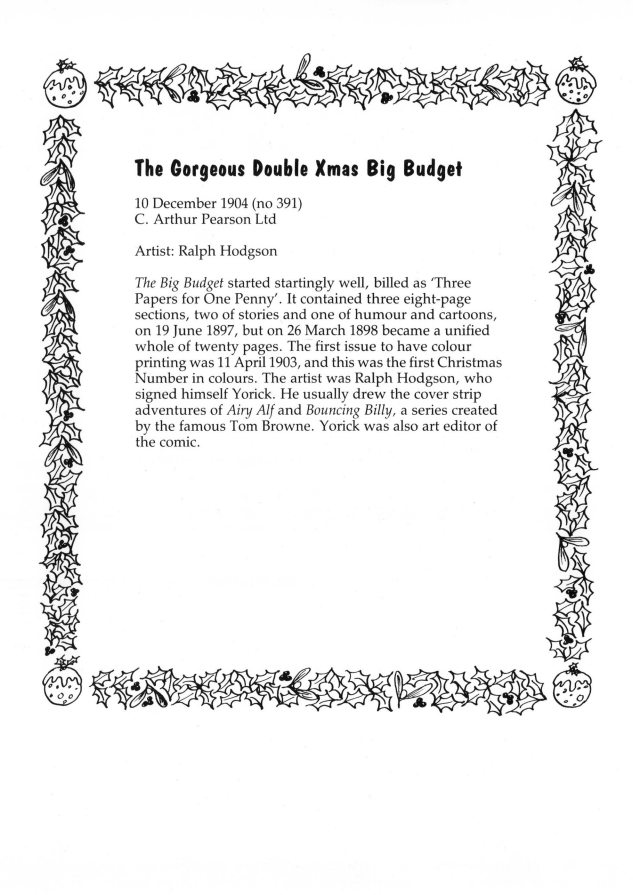

The Gorgeous Double Xmas Big Budget

10 December 1904 (no 391)
C. Arthur Pearson Ltd

Artist: Ralph Hodgson

The Big Budget started startingly well, billed as 'Three Papers for One Penny'. It contained three eight-page sections, two of stories and one of humour and cartoons, on 19 June 1897, but on 26 March 1898 became a unified whole of twenty pages. The first issue to have colour printing was 11 April 1903, and this was the first Christmas Number in colours. The artist was Ralph Hodgson, who signed himself Yorick. He usually drew the cover strip adventures of *Airy Alf* and *Bouncing Billy,* a series created by the famous Tom Browne. Yorick was also art editor of the comic.

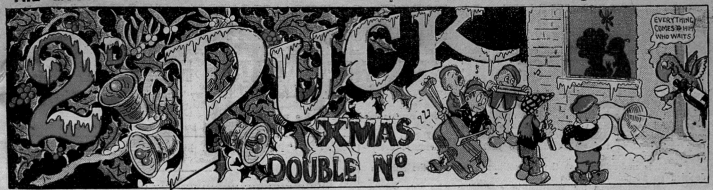

No. 125. Vol. V.   PUBLISHED EVERY FRIDAY.   December 15th, 1906.

OUR MERRY CASEY BOYS ARE FULL OF FUN THIS CHRISTMAS.

1. "I feel a perfect bubble of ideas," said Newlywed to his dear little wifie. "I'll give all the millionaires in Park Lane socks, and a nice little prize packet with a Casey Court boy inside as a Christmas supplement." Hist, dear reader! Anyone about? No! Here's a secret, then! Newlywed is going to let the Caseyites down the chimneys of Park Lane, so that the owners will adopt them. Great scheme, isn't it? Good luck to them in their new homes!

2. Here is Newlywed on the roof-top of Park Lane. "Mind you don't get stuck half way," said he, as he let down Willie Wagstaff. "I expect I shall get a wash here," the youngster warbled back. "They're sure to be rich enough to afford soap, in spite of the Trust. Anyhow, while there's life there's soap, so why worry?"

3. But Newlywed's plan fell through. The millionaires were not taking any, and the Casey Court boys got the Frosty Order of the Boot from the Park Lane flunkeys, all except Lucky Jim. He came off all right. The Dook of Mugwump adopted him.

4. The Dook's page-boy had got the pip stoning so many plums for the Christmas puddings, and had thrown up his job in consequence. So Jimmy was engaged in his place—Lucky Jim! But the change in Jim's behaviour towards his late friends when they called round later as waits was most marked.

5. The Casey boys didn't like to be turned away, and told Jimmy so in a determined tone of voice. "Stop it!" yelled the dook, "fetch the ambulance somebody!"

6. Then Lucky Jim was carried in and given all the best things in the pantry, whilst the Caseyites looked on in disgust from outside. "'E always was lucky," growled Willie Wagstaff. "I s'pose he'll change his front name to Cuthbert now," sniffed Billy Baggs. "These haristocrats ought to be put down by Act of Parliament!"

Puck Xmas Double Number

15 December 1906 (no 125)
B.W. Young (Harmsworth Brothers)

Artist: H. O'Neill

Puck, first published in 30 July 1904, was billed as the first weekly comic to be regularly printed in colours. Unfortunately this was historically incorrect – a typical piece of Alfred Harmsworth promotion! Once again the London Colour Printing Company did the work, showing marked improvement on their colour editions of Harmsworth's other comics in the previous century. The front page strip is adapted from Julius Stafford Baker's *Casey Court* series which had been running in *Illustrated Chips* since 1902. In this Christmas adventure, cartoonist H. O'Neill introduces *The Newlyweds*, ripped off from the American newspaper strip by George McManus.

1d Lot-o'-Fun XMAS

Vol. VIII. No. 198.   December 25th, 1909.   Price ONE PENNY.

Dreamy Has a Right Merry Christmas.

HAPPY XMAS.

TOYS

GEO DAVEY.

1. Ha, ha! a happy Christmas to all of you, dear readers—also the same to me, and many of 'em. Our old pal was hipped, beastly hipped, this festive season, and began to be afraid he was going to have a rotten time of it, don'tcherknow. Absolutely bored. When suddenly—most remarkable thing!—he found himself surrounded by all kinds of toys, all alive and kicking, and they told him he was Father Christmas! 2. And a little later sure enough he *was* that identical old sport, sailing round the sky in a reindeer sledge. "Crumbs," says Dreamy, "if my old club-mates see me in this outfit they'll think I've got a job at Barnum's menagerie. Kim up!" 3. "Although, mind you, I don't reckon I'll ever get all this job done in a single night. If I do I ought to get overtime, that's all." Well, readers, he had just commenced to fill the stockings when— 4. Bang! down fell the top brick off the chimney, and he *woke up!* Sorry to sell you once more; and a Happy New Year, in case we don't see you till next week. Toodle-oo!

Lot-O'-Fun Grand Christmas Double Number

25 December 1909 (no 198)
James Henderson & Sons

Artist: George Davey

Lot-O'-Fun was the first weekly coloured comic to be published by Alfred Harmsworth's chief rival in the field, James Henderson. It started on 17 March 1906 and cost half the price of Harmsworth's *Puck,* one halfpenny. Henderson was playing the Harmsworth touch on the old maestro himself! George Davey, an excellent artist, excelled in his front page series, *Dreamy Daniel,* a tramp who went to sleep every week and had adventures with all kinds of contemporary personalities, even film stars. Once again, the colour printing is by the ubiquitous London Colour Printing Company.

GRAND CHRISTMAS DOUBLE NUMBER.

CHRISTMAS NUMBER 1910.
COMIC-LIFE.
1D · 1D

No. 652. THE RED LIONS HOLD UP FATHER CHRISTMAS. December 17, 1910.

1. It was a high-flown notion, but then our Red Lion Scouts are nothing if not ambitious. "What—waylay Father Christmas, climb up the old fir tree, and pretend to be Christmas ornaments? Our part of speech!" they bleated. "Nothing else," replied Punch Baker, their leader.   2. So up they shinned, and made a pretty picture in the winter landscape, as they unfurled their Union Jacks of old England. Suddenly muffled footsteps sounded o'er the snow-clad scene. "Hush! It isn't my father—it's Father Christmas!" whispered Punch.   3. "Let's hold him up!" "Let's!" replied the scouts. Their brainy leader showed them how to tie their flags to form an aeroplane, and they fluttered down to the dear old toff.   4. "You want what I've got in my sack? Certainly!" smiled the old smiler, and he must have punctured the gasworks, for a terrific bust-up rent the atmosphere!   5. And when our brave boys had come to themselves they found Mr. Baker, and not Father Christmas, standing there. The sack was nothing but a big airball filled with smoke, which hung about just long enough for Punch's father to effect a quick change. How the old Scoutmaster did laugh when he heard it!

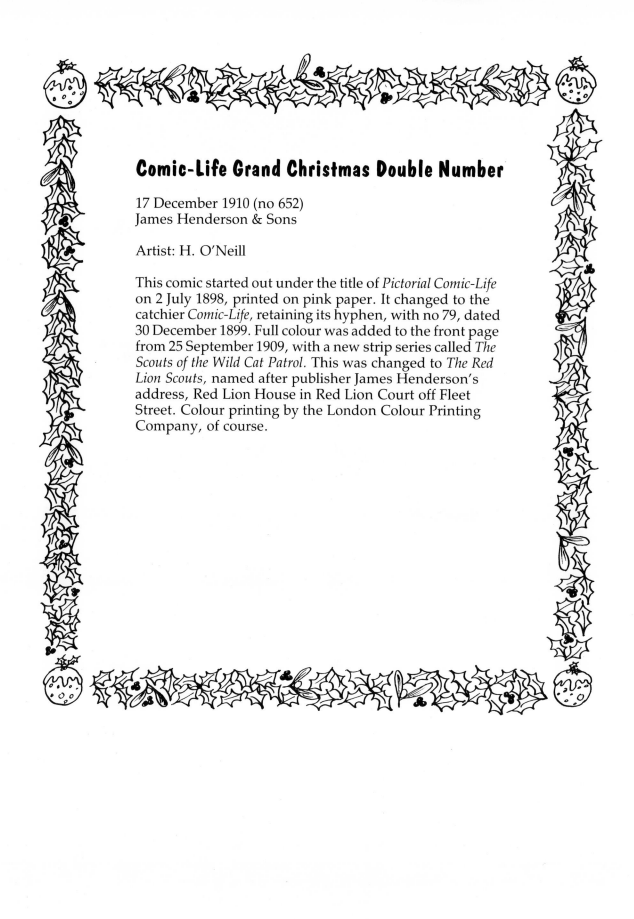

Comic-Life Grand Christmas Double Number

17 December 1910 (no 652)
James Henderson & Sons

Artist: H. O'Neill

This comic started out under the title of *Pictorial Comic-Life* on 2 July 1898, printed on pink paper. It changed to the catchier *Comic-Life*, retaining its hyphen, with no 79, dated 30 December 1899. Full colour was added to the front page from 25 September 1909, with a new strip series called *The Scouts of the Wild Cat Patrol*. This was changed to *The Red Lion Scouts,* named after publisher James Henderson's address, Red Lion House in Red Lion Court off Fleet Street. Colour printing by the London Colour Printing Company, of course.

OUR BUMPER CHRISTMAS NUMBER!

No. 151. Vol. 3. PRICE ONE PENNY. November 25th, 1916.

THE FUNNY ADVENTURES OF BREEZY BEN AND DISMAL DUTCHY ON JUNGLE ISLAND.

1. "Just look at those kids!" said Breezy Ben. "That's an artful fix-up to learn skating with—what? It just lifts the biscuit—doesn't it?" "Vell, vell, I neffer vos!" gurgled Dutchy. "Dey mean to 'ave some pleasurement dis Christmas. Vot about us?"

2. "Quite so, mate!" replied Ben. "Come out of it you lot, and let your elders have a cut! You've been trouble enough to us, in all conscience, this year!" "I don't tink I'll enter for der skating championship yet; put I'm gedding petter!" panted Dutchy.

3. And soon they got going fine. "An hour or two of this will give us enough appetite to eat all the Christmas dinner ourselves," said Ben. "I'll never live to see this through!" groaned Pongo, in agony; while the youngsters kept up a howling accompaniment.

4. But Pongo did "see it through." Oh, yes, it went through all right! You see Ben and Dutchy had cut clean through the ice, and down they splashed into the damp depths. "Just wish all the stewed eels an 'appy Christmas from me!" roared Pongo.

5. But, after all, it was Christmas-time, and Breezy Ben and Dutchy had a soft spot under their waistcoats for the nippers. So after splashing out, they dried themselves, and fixing the only two pairs of skates they had on to two planks, they took out the whole crowd for a skate on the wholesale plan. "Ready?" shouted Ben. "Then go! Left, right, left, right! Jumping Christmas puddings! What fun! Keep it going, lads! Three cheers for the man who invented ice! Right, left! Hooray!"

Chuckles Grand Christmas Number

25 November 1916 (no 151)
Amalgamated Press

Artist: Tom Wilkinson

Chuckles was the first Harmsworth comic in colour to sell at one halfpenny, designed to challenge the two James Henderson comics. The colour printing was by Harmsworth's own press, which helped keep printing costs down. The first issue was published on 10 January 1914, and the usual eight pages per ha'penny was changed to twelve pages for one penny for this Christmas number. *The Funny Adventures of Breezy Ben and Dismal Dutchy on Jungle Island* was drawn by the comic veteran Tom Wilkinson. From 31 May 1919 this knockabout strip changed in style to adapt to a new policy of nursery readership, diluting Wilkinson's wonderful slapstick.

1917 GRAND CHRISTMAS NUMBER

THE RAINBOW 2D

HOORAY FOR FATHER CHRISTMAS.

GPO

A JOLLY XMAS

No. 201. Vol. 4.

" Hip-hip-hurrah ! Three cheers for Father Christmas !" cried the
jolly Bruin Boys, joining hands. "Here we go round the Christmas
Tree !" And what a lot of toys they had ! "I'd like a trumpet,
please !" said Jacko. Mrs. Bruin came in just in time for some presents as well !

December 15, 1917.

The Rainbow Grand Christmas Number

15 December 1917 (no 201)
Amalgamated Press

Artist: Herbert Foxwell

The Rainbow was perhaps Harmsworth's most successful pre-war comic. It was aimed at the nursery reader and starred the famous and already popular team of *Tiger Tim and the Bruin Boys* on the coloured cover. Created by Julius Stafford Baker, this gang of eight was later taken over by Herbert Foxwell, who rapidly rose to the top as favourite nursery artist in children's comics. Usually a six-picture set, this large Christmas illustration was something special.

Merry Moments

CHRISTMAS NUMBER

No. 37. VOL. 1.   EVERY MONDAY.   DECEMBER 20, 1919.

PROFESSOR CRAZY KLEW COMES DOWN THE CHIMNEY AS WELL AS FATHER CHRISTMAS!

1. Cyril and Gladys were having a merry Christmas party. Suddenly, who should come down the chimney but Father Christmas himself! The children were ever so delighted to see him! "Oh, Father Christmas!" cried Gladys, "Do please show us how you get down the chimney." "Why, certainly," chuckled jolly old Father Christmas. "Come on to the roof with me, children!" And he took them up and showed them how big the opening was!

2. But just look who it is peeping at Father Christmas. None other than Professor Crazy Klew—still looking for mysteries! "Who's that old chap on the roof?" he murmured to himself. "He looks like a burglar to me, and as if he's going to climb down the chimney and burgle the house!" Crazy Klew made a great big snowball, and crept stealthily across the roof. "Now to surprise him in the act!" he exclaimed excitedly.

3. Whizz! Crazy Klew hurled the snowball at poor old Father Christmas, and hit him right on the head. "Got you!" cried Crazy Klew joyously. "That'll teach you to burgle at Christmas time!" Poor Father Christmas was so astonished that he lost his footing, and fell down the chimney much quicker than he had intended. "Now you've done it, Professor!" cried Cyril. "Father Christmas won't give you any presents this year!"

4. "Oh, dear!" gasped Crazy Klew. "Was that really Father Christmas?" "Yes, you silly!" cried Cyril. "And you've knocked him down the chimney!" "Then I'll go to his rescue!" declared Crazy Klew. "Help me down after him, children!" Cyril and Gladys grasped Crazy Klew, and bundled him head-first into the chimney opening. "Hurry up, or you'll never catch him!" laughed Cyril.

5. Everybody at the party was very surprised to see Father Christmas come down the chimney again! "Mind yourselves, children!" he gasped. "I can hear somebody else following in my footsteps!"

6. Next moment Professor Crazy Klew himself whizzed into the fireplace, and the Naughty Twins caught him. "So that's the fellow, is it!" laughed Father Christmas. "I thought he was a Christmas ghost!"

7. Soon, however, the party was in full and merry swing again, and they all had a really jolly time. Crazy Klew and Father Christmas became fine friends, and Gladys declared it the nicest Christmas of all!

Merry Moments Christmas Number

20 December 1919 (no 37)
George Newnes Ltd

Artist: unknown

The first regular comic from publisher George Newnes of *Tit-Bits* fame, *Merry Moments* started on 12 April 1919 and ran 194 issues. This is the comic's first Christmas number and as usual the cover star is *Professor Crazy Klew*, a top-hatted detective, with his young chums, *Cyril* and *Gladys*. The artist is unknown, unfortunately, and he seems to have drawn no other comic work. Colour printing by Richard Clay & Sons, Brunswick Street, London SE1.

ALLY SLOPER

THREEPENCE

XMAS NUMBER

CHRISTMAS 1922.

Ally Sloper Xmas Number

December 1922
The Sloperies

Artist: W. F. Thomas

One of the earliest regular comics, *Ally Sloper's Half-Holiday*
started on 3 May 1884. The original series finally packed
up on 9 September 1916, and this, the only coloured
Christmas number, belongs to the new series which ran
from 5 November 1922 for another 97 issues. The
cartoonist who drew this cover was W. F. Thomas, who
had been drawing *The Eminent* for forty years. Throughout
Sloper's long lifetime this remained a comic for adults.

JUNGLE JINKS 2d **GRAND CHRISTMAS NUMBER!**

No. 54. Vol. 3. EVERY THURSDAY. PRICE TWOPENCE. December 13th, 1924.

JOYFUL JINKS ON JUNGLE ISLAND!

1. 'Twas Christmas Eve. Pongo, Porko, Muffins, Tigie, and the other Playmates had gone to their bedroom. Good old Breezy Ben was in the next room when Sambo appeared. "No, Sambo," said Ben in reply to the darky cook, "I will be Father Christmas!"

2. When Sambo had withdrawn, Ben settled himself in an armchair. "I'll just have forty winks," yawned he, "and then I'll visit the boys. The cherubs have all hung their pillowcases on the bed!" Meantime, the cherubs were hatching a deep, dark plot.

3. While Ben was sleeping peacefully, Pongo went into his room and rubbed burnt cork all over his face. As this was being done, Tigie and Muffins brought the full-length looking-glass and stood it in the doorway of Breezy Ben's apartment. "What fun!" tittered Porko.

4. Then the Playmates hid themselves, and Pongo made a noise like a Christmas turkey to wake Ben up. Of course, the first thing Ben saw was himself in the looking-glass. "Sambo!" cried he. "How dare you dress up like that?" *(Continued on the back page.)*

OUR "CIGARETTE PICTURES" — FLAGS SERIES SEE PAGE 10

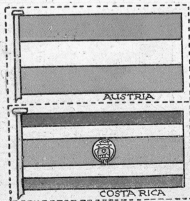
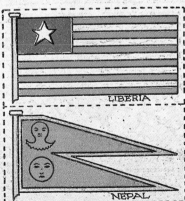
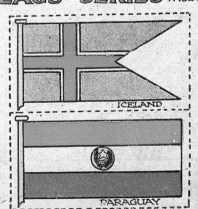

Jungle Jinks Grand Christmas Number

13 December 1924 (no 54)
Amalgamated Press

Artist: Tom Wilkinson

Jungle Jinks was the comic paper which was born out of *Chuckles* (see poster number ten). *Chuckles* was discontinued from 1 December 1923, and *Jungle Jinks* was born on 8 December 1923. This strip, *Joyful Jinks on Jungle Island* is actually a continuation of the first comic's front page stars, *Breezy Ben and Dismal Dutchy*, but is now dominated by an animal gang consisting of *Tigie* (a *Tiger Tim* clone), *Muffins, Pongo* and *Porko*. The cartoonist remains the same, but his style has grown feebler with the passing years.

Tiger Tim's Weekly

No. 163

2ᵈ

Dec. 27th, 1924.

CHRISTMAS NUMBER.

THE BUMPTY BOYS & SANTA CLAUS

1. When Santa Claus came to the Bumpty Boys he did not know they were hiding behind the door.

2. And they caught his coat. "Ha, ha, Santa Claus!" they cried. "You didn't expect to find us awake, did you?" And Santa was so surprised.

3. And he dropped two little trucks out of his sack, and without knowing it, he put his feet in them. "Let me go, boys!" he said. "Oh, no!" laughed Dumpty.

What excitement there was when the Bruin Boys saw their Christmas-tree this year! Porky-boy was so anxious to get at a box of chocolates from the tree that he got all mixed up with the steps. "There ought to be a ship for me somewhere!" said Tim, climbing up; but he pulled over the tree, and wasn't Mrs. Bruin cross!

4. But the trucks on wheels helped Santa to run away. And the Bumpty Boys held on. "Goodness, isn't he going fast!" cried Humpty. "Where do you think he will take us, boys?" "Oh! Oh!" cried Billy Bunny.

5. Presently they came to a dark cave. "Oh!" gasped the boys. "We don't want to go in there! Are you cross with us, Santa?" But the jolly old gentleman he only laughed at them as went in.

6. But they were pleased afterwards, for it was Santa Claus' cave where he kept all his toys. "You aren't afraid now, boys, are you?" he said. "Help yourselves!" And they did. Wasn't that jolly!

Tiger Tim's Weekly Christmas Number

27 December 1924 (no 163)
Amalgamated Press

Artists: Herbert Foxwell, Freddie Crompton

Tiger Tim was such a success in *The Rainbow*, that his
publisher gave him his own weekly comic as well. *Tiger
Tim's Weekly* started on 31 January 1920, but had an earlier
false start as a small oblong paper called *Tiger Tim's Tales*,
1 June 1919. This comic coexisted with *Rainbow* until
18 May 1940, when wartime conditions forced a merger.
The usual *Tim* artist, Herbert Foxwell, drew the large
panel, while Freddie Crompton drew the strip about *The
Bumpty Boys*.

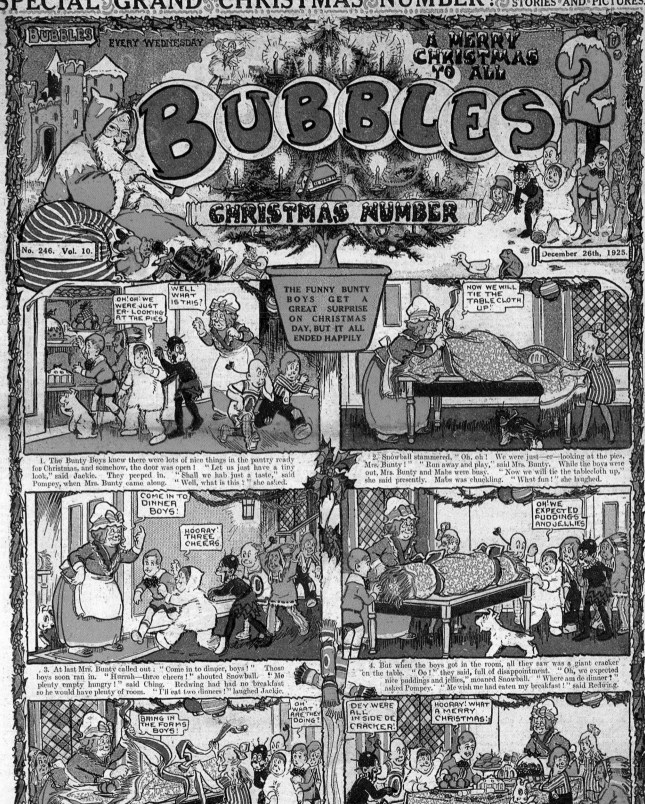

No. 246. Vol. 10.   December 26th, 1925.

THE FUNNY BUNTY BOYS GET A GREAT SURPRISE ON CHRISTMAS DAY, BUT IT ALL ENDED HAPPILY

1. The Bunty Boys knew there were lots of nice things in the pantry ready for Christmas, and somehow, the door was open! "Let us just have a tiny look," said Jackie. They peeped in. "Shall we hab just a taste," said Pompey, when Mrs. Bunty came along. "Well, what is this?" she asked.

2. Snowball stammered, "Oh, oh! We were just—er—looking at the pies, Mrs. Bunty!" "Run away and play," said Mrs. Bunty. While the boys were out, Mrs. Bunty and Mabs were busy. "Now we will tie the tablecloth up," she said presently. Mabs was chuckling. "What fun!" she laughed.

3. At last Mrs. Bunty called out: "Come in to dinner, boys!" Those boys soon ran in. "Hurrah—three cheers!" shouted Snowball. "Me plenty empty hungry!" said Ching. Redwing had had no breakfast so he would have plenty of room. "I'll eat two dinners!" laughed Jackie.

4. But when the boys got in the room, all they saw was a giant cracker on the table. "Oo!" they said, full of disappointment. "Oh, we expected nice puddings and jellies," moaned Snowball. "Where am de dinner?" asked Pompey. "Me wish me had eaten my breakfast!" said Redwing.

5. Mrs. Bunty laughed, and said: "Bring in the forms, boys!" Then she and Mabs untied the ribbons at the ends of the giant cracker, and unrolled the tablecloth. "There's nothing to eat inside crackers!" mumbled Hans. "Hallo, what are they doing?" said Jackie.

6. For when the cracker was opened, there was the Christmas dinner! "Three cheers! The Christmas dinner was there all the time!" said Hans, seating himself near the pudding. "Please I want a lot of everything!" laughed Snowball. They all laughed! (More next week!)

Bubbles Christmas Number

26 December 1925 (no 246)
Amalgamated Press

Artist: Herbert Foxwell

Bubbles began life as a slightly religious Sunday comic entitled *The Children's Fairy*, but it was not successful until it changed both name and publication day (to Wednesday). Herbert Foxwell, busier than ever, added *The Bunty Boys*, star pupils of *Mrs Bunty's Boarding School*, to the front page during 1921, and the comic ran for another twenty years. Each boy came from a different country, including *Snowball the Eskimo*, *Ching the Chinese boy*, *Pompey the African*, *Redwing the American Indian*, and, of course, *Jackie the Brit*.

Jolly Christmas Cards to Send to Your Friends

(SEE BACK PAGE.)

THE CHICKS' OWN 2ᴰ

No. 325.   Dec. 18th, 1926.

Rupert the Chick's Christ-mas Pud-ding—don't you wish you had it?

The Chicks' Own

18 December 1926 (no 325)
Amalgamated Press

Artist: Arthur White

The Chicks' Own was hatched on 25 September 1920, originally starring *Dicky the Duck.* One year later a more suitable front page hero was introduced, *Rupert the Chick,* drawn by the same artist, Arthur White, who would continue to illustrate *Rupert's* adventures for some 37 years. Usually starring in a four or six picture strip, this Christmas number featured a special large picture cover cartoon. The editor was Langton Townley, who under the alias of *Uncle Dan* wishes all his Chicks a Mer-ry Christ-mas (the comic was hyphenated for young readers) and Heaps of Pud!

No. 265. New Series.   EVERY WEDNESDAY.   December 22nd, 1928

TEDDY AND TILDA AND MRS. WHISKERS' SCAMPS.

1. It was Christmas Eve, and Teddy and Tilda and the scamps were out doing their Christmas shopping. "That is the tree we'll have," said Len Lion. "It's a beauty!"

2. But just then they saw a poor old man singing carols in the street. "Oh, let's give him our money!" cried Tilda. "We'll do without our Christmas tree this year!"

3. Of course, the poor old man was delighted with the money. "You are indeed kind," said he. "Here is a magic bean. Plant it, to-morrow it will be a tree!"

4. "Whoops! He's given Teddy a wonderful bean!" cried Len. And they all dashed home to plant that lucky bean in Mrs. Whiskers' best pot.

5. And would you believe it? When they came down on Christmas morning they found that bean had grown into the loveliest Christmas tree you ever saw! "See! This is what comes of doing a kind action!" said Mrs. Whiskers, as she came in with the steaming plum pudding. "Here's wishing you all a very merry Christmas!"

Playtime Grand Xmas Number

22 December 1928 (no 265)
Amalgamated Press

Artist: George Jones

Playtime started on 29 March 1919 as the first small format coloured comic, twenty-four pages for two pence. Despite being extremely attractive, with some of the best cartoonists of the period, it was not a great success and from 24 November 1923 it began again with a new series, at number one. This time it was in traditional tabloid format and editor Frank Anderson modelled it on *The Rainbow*, bringing in George Jones to draw a typical nursery-appeal front page entitled *Teddy and Tilda and Mrs Whiskers' Scamps*. The *Scamps* were the usual merry menagerie: *Len Lion, Neddy Donkey, Foxy, Piggy,* and *Toddles* and *Teedles*, the pup and the kitten.

Grand Christmas Number

No. 205.] **MOLLY AND THE MERRY MIDDIES!** [December 26th, 1931.

THE playmates were so excited when they woke up on Christmas Morning, and found their stockings crammed with toys. When they had looked at them all, Molly said : "Now let us dress and go down and see our real presents." "Merry Christmas, Captain !" they cried. But they did get a shock when Captain said : "No presents for you ! Tidy up this playroom."

2. And with that out went Captain. "How mean of him," said Monty. "Oh, well, never mind," said Teddy. "Let's get it done, and then go out and build a snowman. Open that cupboard, Tim, and I'll get this lot inside." But when Tim opened that cupboard, there were shrieks of delight as the playmates saw all those lovely toys. "They're our presents from Captain and Tom," cried Molly.

3. Never had the chums had such wonderful presents, and when they'd looked at them all, they ran off to thank Captain and Thomas. And after that, a great deal of whispering went on among the playmates, after which, they ran off to the garden, and began to build their snowmen. "Hurry up, boys," said Molly. "Captain and Thomas will be along soon, and we've got a lot to do."

4. They all worked with a will, and soon they'd made a couple of snowmen that were the exact images of Captain and Thomas. Just as they had finished, Monty whispered : "Here they come ! Let's hide, chums !" So indoors they ran. "Well, I never !" cried the captain. "The ungrateful little rascals, making fun of us like this, after all those lovely presents we've given them."

5. And the grown-ups were so angry that they seized the rake and shovel, and started to attack the offending snowmen. Over they toppled, and then Captain and Thomas got a surprise as they saw two huge boxes, labelled, "To Captain, with love," and "To Thomas, with love." "Well, I never !" beamed Cappy. "These are their presents to us, the little dears." "Oooh !" smiled Thomas delightedly. "Let's hurry and open them, shall we, Cap'n ?" And as they started to open the boxes, the playmates chorused : "Merry Christmas, everyone."

6. It was a merry Christmas, too ! Cappy had provided a wonderful dinner. "Three cheers for Captain !" cried the chums, as Captain Hearty carved the turkey. When it came to the holly-trimmed plum pudding, everyone found a lucky silver present in their portion. After dinner there were games and dancing in the playroom, and, after that, a huge Christmas-tree. And— "We've never had such a Christmas !" declared the chums as they trooped off happily to bed. And we hope you'll all have the same, readers.

2000

My Favourite Grand Christmas Number

26 December 1931 (no 205)
Amalgamated Press

Artist: William Wakefield

My Favourite started on 28 January 1928, growing out of the old weekly, *Comic Life.* One of the few comics to be edited by a woman, Florence Pearce gradually turned this paper into a vehicle for picture serials rather than funnies, although the front cover always remained humorous. This was drawn with great neatness and care by George William 'Billy' Wakefield, the great cartoonist who drew Laurel and Hardy for *Film Fun* for so many years. *My Favourite* ran for 351 issues, closing on 13 October 1934.

"THE SUNBEAM" 2D.

THE SUNBEAM

GRAND CHRISTMAS NUMBER

2D

No. 309.]   THE MISCHIEFS HAVE A MERRY CHRISTMAS.   [January 2nd, 1932.

DEAR BOYS AND GIRLS,—The Mischiefs were very good at Christmas time, and as they are too modest to write and tell you about it themselves, I am going to do it this week. They had been to town to buy some toys, when they saw a poor crossing-sweeper.

2. She was too poor to buy her children any Christmas toys, and the boys felt very sorry for her. They made up their minds to give the poor children those they had bought. But, first of all, they put the crossing-sweeper's broom in a flower-pot filled with snow.

3. Then they tied the toys on to the bristles of the broom so that it looked like a big Christmas tree. What a lovely treat it was for those poor little children. "The toys are all for you," the mischiefs said. It made them so happy to see how delighted the poor children were with the toys. "Bless you, kind children !" said the old crossing-sweeper.

4. Then the boys went back to school and, as it was not quite bedtime, they had a jolly game of snowballs in the playground. Even dog Toby joined in the fun. I am glad I wasn't there, though, for I am sure they would have snowballed me just like they did Simple Simon. But he gave them as good as they sent, and the fun grew fast and furious.

5. Very soon there were snowballs sticking all over the school wall and, do you know, those snowballs formed into words, and the words they made were " A Merry Xmas." Just as the Mischiefs were laughing at what had happened, Mother Hubbard popped out and reminded them that it was bedtime—time for them to hang up their stockings.

6. The boys did not need telling twice and, later, when they were all fast asleep, Santa Claus came along and saw the snowball greeting. "Ah ! a Christmas card for me," he said. "I must pick them out some extra nice toys ! " And he did. So the boys were rewarded for their kindness, and had a lovely Christmas.—Your affectionate, UNCLE JACK.

(Another adventure of the Merry Mischiefs in the New Year Number of "Sunbeam" on sale Saturday, January 2nd, 1932.)

The Sunbeam Grand Christmas Number

2 January 1932 (no 309)
Amalgamated Press

Artist: Freddie Crompton

The Sunbeam was another long-running comic weekly whose life divided in two parts. It started on 7 October 1922, taking over from the unsuccessful *Little Sparks*, then started again on 30 January 1926 with a new series. Its total run when the comic wound up on 25 May 1940 was 920 issues. The famous front page strip, *Mother Hubbard's Merry Mischiefs*, began with the new series, and featured a happy host of nursery rhyme characters, including *Humpty Dumpty*, *Tom the Piper's son*, *Simple Simon* and *Georgie Porgie*, delightfully drawn by Frederick 'Freddie' Crompton.

A HAPPY CHRISTMAS TO ALL OUR READERS.

Bo-Peep and Little Boy Blue

24 December 1932 (no 167)
Amalgamated Press

Artist: unknown

Rising out of the ashes of *Playtime* came this new nursery comic, *Bo-Peep and Little Boy Blue*, born 19 October 1929. Unfortunately the artist selected by editor Frank Anderson to draw the front page series has not been identified. *Bo-Peep* herself supposedly wrote the weekly editorial, and in this special issue she says, 'I hope all your puddings will be big ones, all your mince pies have sixpences in, and your stocking be filled with all the very things that you had set your heart on!' And so say all of us!

FOR BOYS AND GIRLS
THE CHRISTMAS COMIC
2ᴰ

FATHER CHRISTMAS COMES TO THE PARTY
And So Does a Lovely Snow-man

1. Hurrah ! Father Christmas was coming to the party, and the Jungle Boys were so excited. While Milly and Billy were out of the room they hatched a deep plot to meet Father Christmas directly he arrived and get first pick of the toys.

2. But Milly and Billy had overheard and, laughing, they decided to make a plan of their own. As soon as the time came for Father Christmas to arrive, they built a grand snowman and put a Father Christmas cloak over him.

3. When they had finished, it looked just like Father Christmas himself, and then Billy took the broomstick and placed it between the knocker and the door. He lifted the knocker and gave a resounding bang ! Then he and Milly ran round the corner.

4. The Jungle Boys, all dressed in their best for the great party, were waiting and watching the clock. There came a knock on the front door. It must be Father Christmas. Cheers ! They rushed pell-mell to the door and opened it.

5. Not stopping an instant, they each wanted to be first to greet Father Christmas, and as those behind pushed those in front at the door, poor Father Christmas suddenly fell over and the Jungle Boys flopped in the cold snow. Father Christmas had vanished !

6. How Milly and Billy laughed ! All the time Father Christmas had come in by the big door at the back, as a surprise, and when the Jungle Boys got to their feet, there he was. They chuckled heartily at the joke Milly and Billy had played on them.

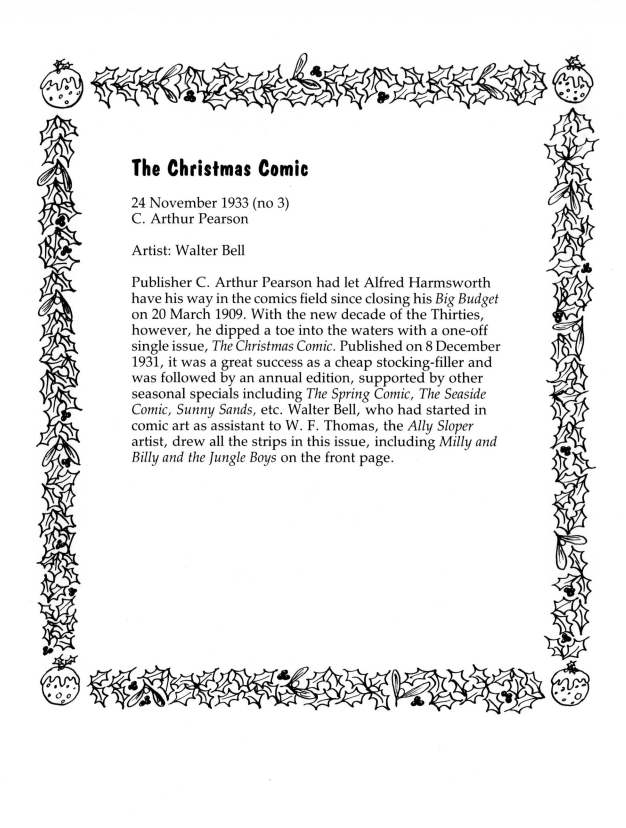

The Christmas Comic

24 November 1933 (no 3)
C. Arthur Pearson

Artist: Walter Bell

Publisher C. Arthur Pearson had let Alfred Harmsworth have his way in the comics field since closing his *Big Budget* on 20 March 1909. With the new decade of the Thirties, however, he dipped a toe into the waters with a one-off single issue, *The Christmas Comic.* Published on 8 December 1931, it was a great success as a cheap stocking-filler and was followed by an annual edition, supported by other seasonal specials including *The Spring Comic, The Seaside Comic, Sunny Sands,* etc. Walter Bell, who had started in comic art as assistant to W. F. Thomas, the *Ally Sloper* artist, drew all the strips in this issue, including *Milly and Billy and the Jungle Boys* on the front page.

Merry and Bright Xmas Fun Number

23 December 1933 (no 872)
Amalgamated Press

Artist: Roy Wilson

The first front page by this cartoonist in this collection, and one of his best – a black-and-white penny comic with all the colour of a two-penny coloured comic. The artist is Royston Warner Wilson, who by the Thirties had risen to become the contemporary King of Comic artists. *Merry and Bright,* edited by Frederick Cordwell, had begun on 22 October 1910, started a second series on 7 April 1917, and finally concluded on 19 January 1935, a total run of 1,265 weekly issues. Always a cheap comic (only a halfpenny when first begun) it had several changes of coloured paper during its run, from blue to pink, yellow and finally mauve.

December 24, 1933—No. 6895.

JOLLY JACK'S WEEKLY

JUNIOR SECTION—SUNDAY DISPATCH

FUN AT MRS. LEO'S CHRISTMAS PARTY

FOXWELL

The merry folk from the Pages of "Jolly Jack's Weekly" come to Mrs. Leo's party.

"Hooray! Here comes the pudding!" cheered the merrymakers at Mrs. Leo's party. "Will one be enough, do you think?" murmured Tubby. "I'd like to lasso a whole one for myself!" "Dear me!" chuckled Professor Simple. "We are having a gay time! I wonder if anyone would kiss me under the mistletoe?" Meanwhile, Jolly Jack and Timothy, the cabin boy, were having great fun with the cubs and a giant cracker. "Why, there's a cuckoo inside!" laughed Jack. "Let's take him back to the Fun Ship and make old Pimple jealous!" Just then Santa Claus arrived to give everybody a Christmas present, and then you may be sure the party went with a swing.

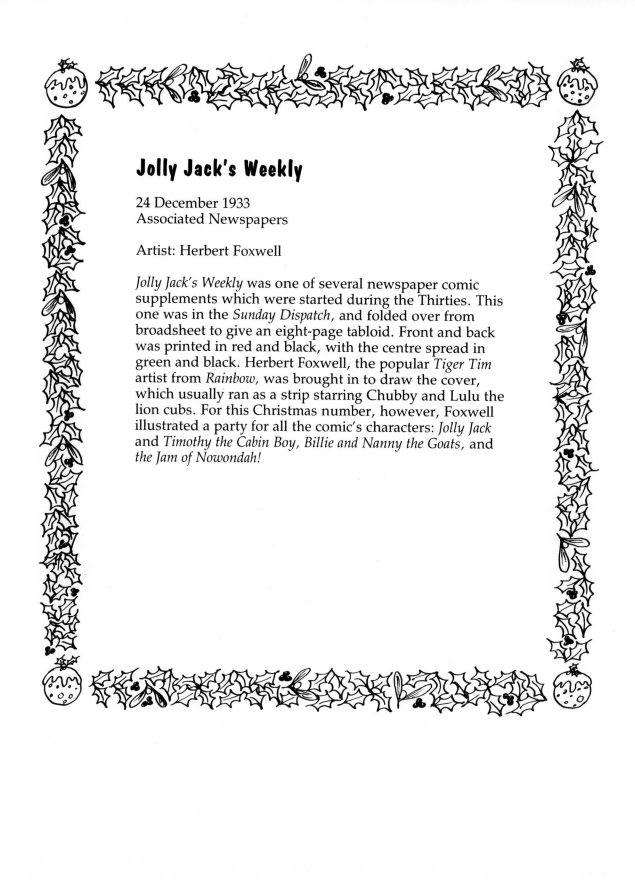

Jolly Jack's Weekly

24 December 1933
Associated Newspapers

Artist: Herbert Foxwell

Jolly Jack's Weekly was one of several newspaper comic supplements which were started during the Thirties. This one was in the *Sunday Dispatch,* and folded over from broadsheet to give an eight-page tabloid. Front and back was printed in red and black, with the centre spread in green and black. Herbert Foxwell, the popular *Tiger Tim* artist from *Rainbow,* was brought in to draw the cover, which usually ran as a strip starring Chubby and Lulu the lion cubs. For this Christmas number, however, Foxwell illustrated a party for all the comic's characters: *Jolly Jack* and *Timothy the Cabin Boy, Billie and Nanny the Goats,* and *the Jam of Nowondah!*

CHRISTMAS CRACKERS

1. Dear Old Chums,—A Merry Christmas to you all! May your stockings overflow, and may you eat Christmas pudding till—— Oh dear! I nearly forgot to tell you about the strange thing that happened to me and my sister Sue on Christmas Eve. We thought we'd catch old Santa Claus with a little trap.

2. You know, I'd got an idea that old Pa was Santa Claus. Mind you, I didn't know, so I wanted to find out. I do know, though, that our chimney isn't large enough for a puss-cat to come down, let alone old Santa. Presently we heard the handle of our bedroom door turned. "Sh! sh! He's coming!" I whispered.

3. In a jiffy me and Sue bobbed down and pretended to be asleep, with one eye open. The door opened, and it stretched the string I had fixed to the water-jug. The next tick there was a howl, and we saw a funny old figure with whiskers dancing around with the jug on his head! "A fine catch that, Sue!" I chuckled.

4. "Who is it?" asked Sue, while I seized the jug and tried to pull the thing off. "I don't know 'xactly, but it sounds like Pa," I said. Now, while we were busy, Ma popped in at the window, and filled our stockings and pillow cases right up to the very top with all kinds of toys and things. We didn't see her, though!

5. The next tick the jolly old water-jug came off Santa's head, and then we saw that it was Pa after all. "There! what did I tell you, Curly?" I cried. "There isn't a Santa Claus—it's only Dad!" Suddenly Sue gave a gasp. "Hey, Big Boy! What about this?" she yelled in great excitement. "Santa's been!"

6. Well, I tell you straight, chums, I didn't know what to make of it. Pa couldn't have been Santa Claus after all, 'cause he hadn't brought any toys. Still, three cheers for Santa, anyway! We had a jolly time with the things he'd brought us, I can tell you. Cheerio!—Your very merry chums, HARRY AND SUE.

Christmas Crackers

30 December 1933 (no 254)
Amalgamated Press

Artist: Roy Wilson

Roy Wilson's second Christmas cover of the year (see *Merry and Bright*) was a full colour celebration of the season, complete with those side-columns of toys, crackers and fruit that were so much a part of Christmas comickery. *Crackers* was edited by Stanley Gooch, and started on 23 February 1929, running to 31 May 1941 when it concluded its run at no 615 as a small sized comic in *Radio Fun* format. *The Jolly Adventures of Happy Harry and Sister Sue* by Wilson started in 1933 and set the middleclass tone of the comic with their homely slapstick capers with *Pa* and *Ma*.

JOLLY JUMBO'S CHRISTMAS HOLIDAY Comic

"SNOW" USE PLAYING TRICKS ON JUMBO
He's Sure to Come Out On Top in the End

1. Jolly Jumbo and his merry friends had been hard at work making some grand toboggans, for it had been snowing hard and the whole world outside was a blanket of white. It was Jolly Jumbo who thought of a race, and Leo said it was a great idea.

2. Up the hill of snow the two teams dragged their toboggans, but—hallo! What was that? One team had noticed the tree stump and they were going to say nothing about it to the other team so that they themselves would win the race.

3. It was unfair of them, and Jolly Jumbo and his crew did not know a thing about what was in store for them. Ah, here were the two toboggans, with Jolly Jumbo's just a wee bit behind. "Look out for bumps!" warned Jolly Jumbo, who was a sport.

4. That naughty crew did not look out for them, however, and suddenly their toboggan hit a wide bump and began to tip over. More and more it tipped, until it had shot its crew right off. And Jolly Jumbo's toboggan was rushing along right behind.

5. At that moment Jolly Jumbo and his men hit the tree stump with a crash that sent them sliding off their toboggan. "Serves you right, Jumbo, for being so clever," cried Jimmy Giraffe unkindly. But Jumbo had been trying to help, hadn't he?

6. Jolly Jumbo's turn was soon to come, for instead of piling up in the snow, he and his men sailed right on to the other crew's toboggan, and away it went to the winning post, with Jolly Jumbo and Co. easy winners. But they deserved to win, didn't they?

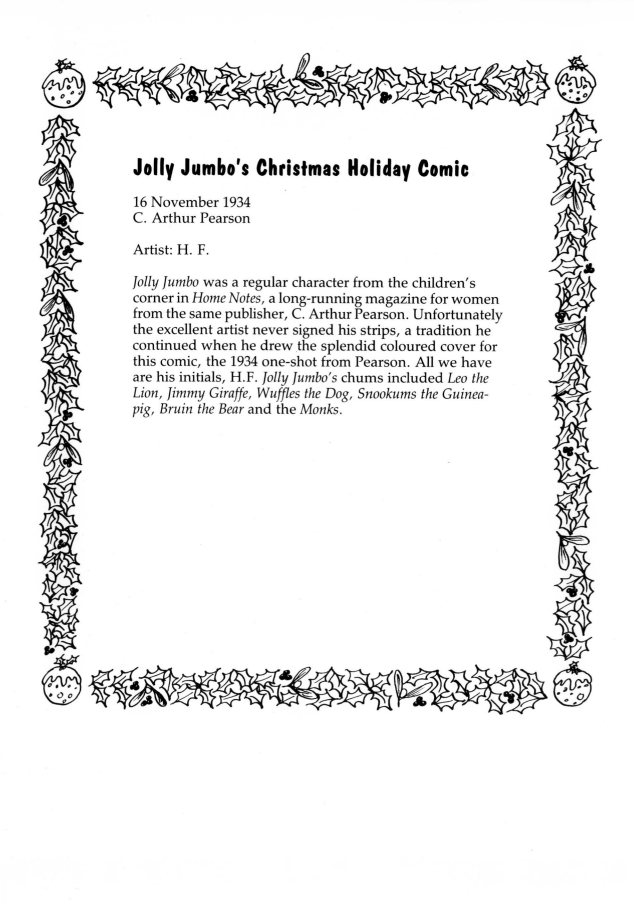

Jolly Jumbo's Christmas Holiday Comic

16 November 1934
C. Arthur Pearson

Artist: H. F.

Jolly Jumbo was a regular character from the children's corner in *Home Notes,* a long-running magazine for women from the same publisher, C. Arthur Pearson. Unfortunately the excellent artist never signed his strips, a tradition he continued when he drew the splendid coloured cover for this comic, the 1934 one-shot from Pearson. All we have are his initials, H.F. *Jolly Jumbo's* chums included *Leo the Lion, Jimmy Giraffe, Wuffles the Dog, Snookums the Guinea-pig, Bruin the Bear* and the *Monks.*

A Merry Christmas to all our Readers

BOYS AND GIRLS

Your Own Picture Paper

Daily Mail

SATURDAY, DECEMBER 22, 1934.

TEDDY TAIL'S CHRISTMAS CALLER

FOXWELL

"HULLO, boys and girls, here we are again," called a jolly voice, and the Whisker Pets raced outside to greet Father Christmas—in an aeroplane! "I should never get round in time in a sleigh, there are so many boys and girls waiting for me!" he explained. "Hurrah for Father Christmas and all his jolly friends," called Teddy Tail, and the Pets hurrahed until they were hoarse! "Thank you!" carolled Cinderella and Dick Whittington. "See you at the pantomime!"

Boys and Girls Daily Mail

22 December 1934
Associated Newspapers

Artist: Herbert Foxwell

Known universally as *The Teddy Tail Comic*, this newspaper supplement started on 8 April 1933 and ran for five years. It was so popular that it appeared twice a week from 26 July 1933, and then thrice a week from 12 September. Starting as black on yellow paper, colour printing (orange on covers, green on centre spreads) began on 3 June 1933, and even special 'Magic Ink' issues were printed later on. The comic doubled in format to huge broadsheet size from 14 September 1935. *Teddy Tail* had been a daily cartoon feature for children in the parent paper since 1915, when it was drawn by Charles Folkard. Herbert Foxwell was brought over from *The Rainbow* to take on the revitalization in 1933.

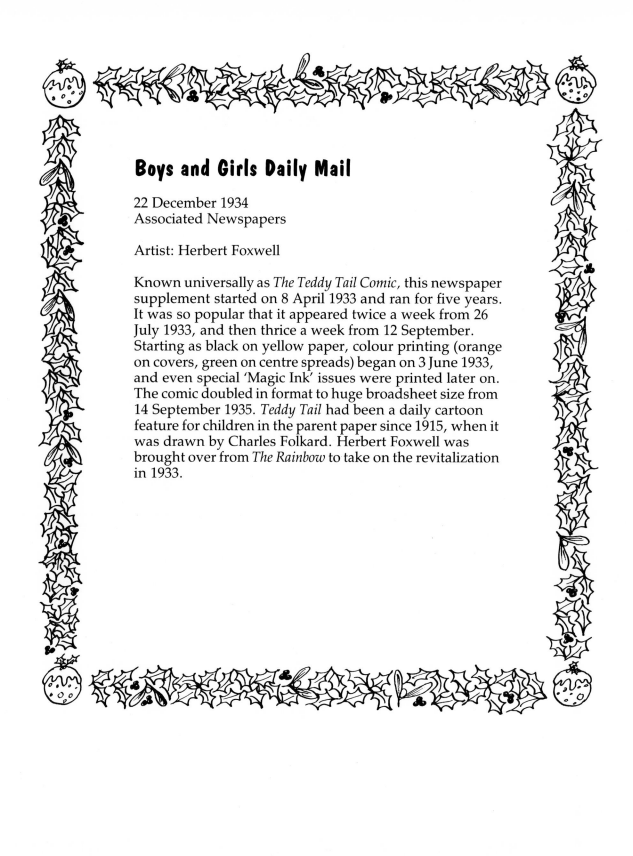

THE SPARKLER 2d

XMAS NUMBER

LIEUTENANT DARING AND JOLLY ROGER, IF YOU PLEASE,
FLY THROUGH THE AIR WITH THE GREATEST OF EASE.

No. 63.]   [December 28th, 1935.

1. It was Christmas Eve, really it was, and all at once there was such an uproar aboard H.M.S. *Joybelle*, anchored off some fine old English port. For all at once two rash rascals swooped down in an aeroplane, lassooed our handsome young Lieutenant Douglas Daring, and whisked him away.

2. Kidnapped on his own quarterdeck, was Doug.! But did that able young seaman, Jolly Roger, stand still and do nowt about it ? He did not ! He hopped on to the big gadget used for catapulting aeroplanes into the sky. "Shoot, shipmates!" roared Roger. "I go to join the guv'nor !"

3. Zun-ng ! went the giant catty, and up into the sky, ever so high, zipped Roger. And on to the wing of the kidnappers' 'plane he dropped. "Don't save yourself, sir !" he yelled. "Please let me rescue you as it's Christmas-time." But the wind carried away his words—ay, all of them.

4. And having by this time been dragged into the cockpit by the nasty chappie, Daring proceeded to let it be known to these sky-pirates that they couldn't do just what they liked with *him*. Oh dear, no ! Which was just what Roger thought as he galloped up the steeply sloping wing

5. It was a hard climb, believe us. But sailors don't care—and they don't give up, either. All at once, though, the aeroplane luffed, heeled over, or—ah, banked, is the word, and Roger suddenly found himself going down instead of up. In fact he dived head-first on to the pilot—

6. And completely bent that gentleman's hair-parting. Then what ? Why, our pocket-sized mariner took charge of the joystick while Doug. battled with the other rascal. "Have this with me !" he cried. Bing ! "And this with the Navy !" Bong ! "And this for a merry Christmas !" Plunk !

7. That settled Mr. Kidnapper. "Belay there !" roared Doug. "Hard a-starboard, Roger !" "Ay, ay, sir !" shouted the small sailor smartly. "But you're too late. We've run aground, sir. Mind the bump ! Whoops !"

8. Strange though it may seem, the aeroplane had run right into the roof of the old ancestral home of Lieutenant Daring. "How's that, sir ?" tweeted Roger. "Do we stay to dinner ?" A pair of policemen soon marched—

9. Off the kidnappers, after which Roger was introduced to the family. But you can take it from me that he enjoyed the introduction to the turkey and the Christmas pudding and other festive trimmings ever so much better !

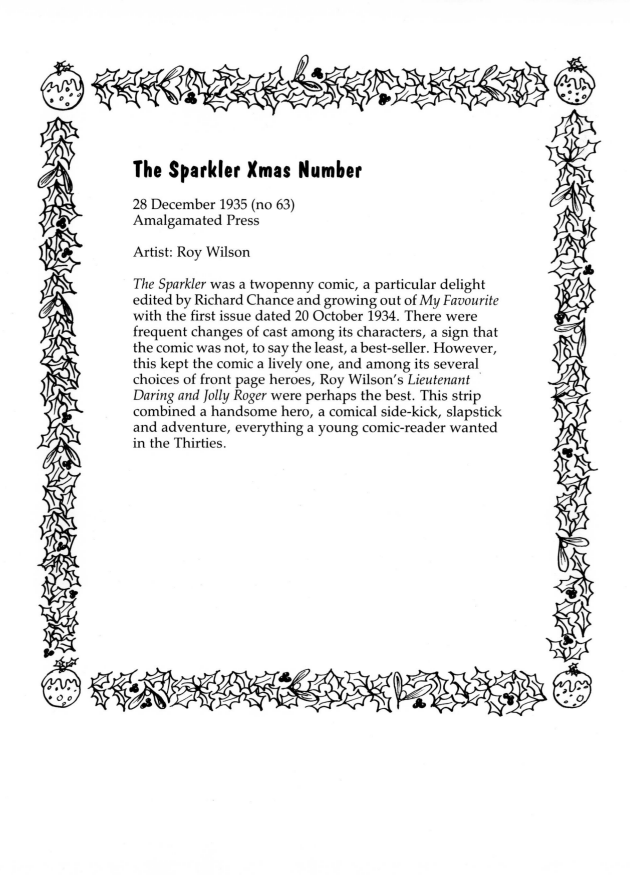

The Sparkler Xmas Number

28 December 1935 (no 63)
Amalgamated Press

Artist: Roy Wilson

The Sparkler was a twopenny comic, a particular delight
edited by Richard Chance and growing out of *My Favourite*
with the first issue dated 20 October 1934. There were
frequent changes of cast among its characters, a sign that
the comic was not, to say the least, a best-seller. However,
this kept the comic a lively one, and among its several
choices of front page heroes, Roy Wilson's *Lieutenant
Daring and Jolly Roger* were perhaps the best. This strip
combined a handsome hero, a comical side-kick, slapstick
and adventure, everything a young comic-reader wanted
in the Thirties.

1. Pop Tiddleywink was busy decorating the jolly old Christmas-tree—and a very posh job he was making of it, too. "Ah!" said Pop, admiring his own handiwork. "Soon be finished now! Just putting the finishing touches to it."

2. Dad Tiddleywink was right when he said "finishing" touches. Yes, he dropped a ball out of the old present box, and when Salmon and Shrimp went racing after it, they cannoned into the ladder. Pop had to grab the tree.

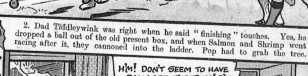

3. Of course, Pop was just a little too much makeweight for that Christmas-tree, and over it went—with the old Tiddleywink daddy on top of it. "Oh dear!" cried Sonny. "That's good-bye to our Christmas-tree! Pop's bent it properly!"

4. Up got Pop and set about sorting himself out from that festive festoonery. "H'm! Sorry, children!" he piped. "Must have trod on a step that wasn't there. But let's have a look at the toys. Perhaps they're not damaged—eh?"

5. Having filled himself up with a double portion of puff mixture, Pop decided to see if a squeaker was bent, busted, or broken. As he leaned out of the window to test that squeaker, Larry Liftem was legging it by with a gent's timepiece.

6. Lo and be bothered if yon end of the jolly old squeaker didn't fasten round that watch-chain, and, on the rebound, whisk both timepiece and chain from the bad lad's handie-pandie. "Oh, bravo, sir!" cried the old gent to Pop.

7. Wasn't the old watch-owner grateful. "Thank you, sir!" he cried. "Now, I'm giving a party at the Manor! Perhaps you'd like to come along—and, of course, bring the family?" "Coo!" cried Sis. "A Christmas-tree treat, after all!"

8. What a lovely party it turned out to be, too! And what a wonderful Christmas-tree they had there. Of course, when there was a game of ring-a-ring o'-roses round it, Pop joined in—but he was careful to watch his step this time!

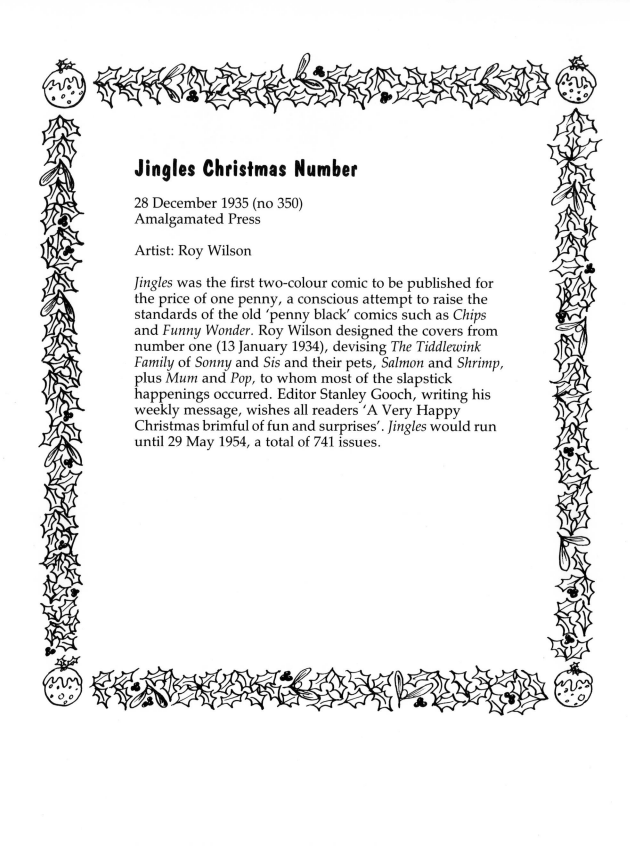

Jingles Christmas Number

28 December 1935 (no 350)
Amalgamated Press

Artist: Roy Wilson

Jingles was the first two-colour comic to be published for the price of one penny, a conscious attempt to raise the standards of the old 'penny black' comics such as *Chips* and *Funny Wonder*. Roy Wilson designed the covers from number one (13 January 1934), devising *The Tiddlewink Family* of *Sonny* and *Sis* and their pets, *Salmon* and *Shrimp*, plus *Mum* and *Pop,* to whom most of the slapstick happenings occurred. Editor Stanley Gooch, writing his weekly message, wishes all readers 'A Very Happy Christmas brimful of fun and surprises'. *Jingles* would run until 29 May 1954, a total of 741 issues.

Tip Top Christmas Number

28 December 1935 (no 89)
Amalgamated Press

Artist: Roy Wilson

Tip Top was the companion comic to *Jingles*, starting 21 April 1934 and closing on the same date as *Jingles*, 29 May 1954, running up a total of 727 editions. It began as a black-and-green comic, changing to the orange tint as shown here, and eventually becoming a full colour comic on 6 January 1940. The cover serial, *'The Adventures of Jerry, Jenny and Joe'*, was created by Reg Parlett, but taken over by Roy Wilson at the instigation of editor Stanley Gooch, a great admirer of Wilson's work. Note how the artist incorporates a traditional English Christmas party into the depths of the African jungle.

FUN AND FROLIC FOR YOUR CHRISTMAS HOLIDAY

MILLY, BILLY AND THE BOYS SING FOR THEIR SUPPER

1. Milly and Billy and the Boys were singing Xmas carols for all they were worth outside Colonel Happyman's house. They hadn't played a wrong note and everything was going with a swing. They were sure that Colonel and Mrs. Happyman were enjoying it.

2. But wait! The bad Benson boys were up to their tricks. They were planning to climb on to the roof of the house and send the snow down in a great heap, right on top of our friends. It would stop the carols and spoil everything. The naughty lads!

3. Up they went, quiet as mice, and nobody heard them. There they perched on the sloping roof, gathering the snow into a pile all ready for the final push. And our friends didn't know a thing about it. It was a shame! Would the plan work? We shall see.

4. All of a sudden Billy happened to look aloft, and what a shock he got! He saw a huge hill of snow slithering to the edge of the roof. Just then out came the Colonel with some cash for their singing. In a second Billy rushed forward—to warn the Colonel.

5. And, instead of taking the cash as the Colonel thought he was going to do, he grabbed his arm. With Milly he rushed him forward away from the porch, where the snow fell with a terrific plomp! But what was that? Why, those lads had fallen, too.

6. You see, as the snow slid over the top, so they went with it, for there was nothing to grab hold of. They didn't hurt themselves, but they got a rare shaking-up. As for our chums, the Colonel was so pleased that he invited them in for his party.

Grand stories, jokes, puzzles, riddles and all sorts of good things inside

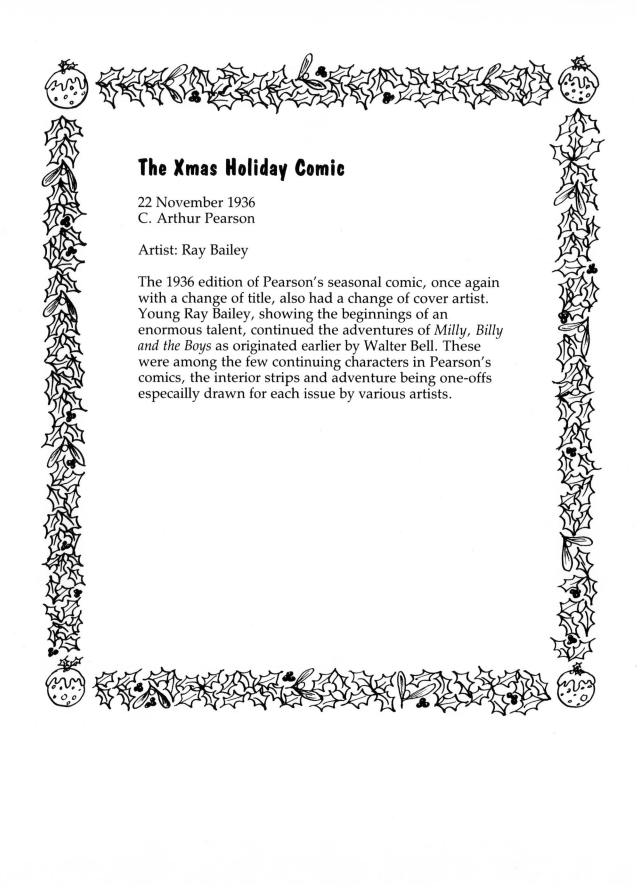

The Xmas Holiday Comic

22 November 1936
C. Arthur Pearson

Artist: Ray Bailey

The 1936 edition of Pearson's seasonal comic, once again
with a change of title, also had a change of cover artist.
Young Ray Bailey, showing the beginnings of an
enormous talent, continued the adventures of *Milly, Billy
and the Boys* as originated earlier by Walter Bell. These
were among the few continuing characters in Pearson's
comics, the interior strips and adventure being one-offs
especailly drawn for each issue by various artists.

TINY TOTS 2D. EVERY THURSDAY

A MERRY CHRISTMAS TO YOU !

Tiny Tots

CHRISTMAS   NUMBER   2D

No. 479. Vol. 19. Every Thursday.   WEEK ENDING December 19th, 1936.

TI-NY AND TOT STIR THE CHRIST-MAS PUD-DING !

1. When Ti-ny and Tot came in-to the kitch-en, they found nur-sie mak-ing the Christ-mas pud-ding-s. Of course, she let the child-ren have a stir for luck, and said they could have one of the pud-ding-s for din-ner.

2. While nur-sie was cook-ing the pud-ding-s, Ti-ny and Tot said they would go out and get some hol-ly. "We must dress up the room for Christ-mas," said Ti-ny. "The pud-ding-s are near-ly done," said nur-sie.

3. While the child-ren were cut-ting the hol-ly, nur-sie dish-ed up the pud-ding-s. "I will mark this one with a cross," she said. "Then I shall know which one has the mon-ey in it, and we can have it for din-ner."

4. Ti-ny and Tot were sur-prise-d when they came in-door-s and saw the cross on the pud-ding. "I ex-pect cook want-s all the oth-er pud-ding-s mark-ed with a cross, as well," said Ti-ny. "I will put cross-es on them."

5. When nur-sie found cross-es on all the pud-ding-s, she did not know which one had the mon-ey in it. "Oh dear, and they are all mix-ed up, too !" she said. "Now what shall I do ? I do not know which one to choose."

6. By good luck nur-sie pick-ed out the right pud-ding, and Ti-ny found a six-pence in his por-tion and Tot one in her-s. Of course, they were de-light-ed. "Hoo-ray !" cried Tiny. "I am glad we both had a stir !"

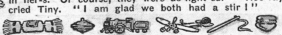

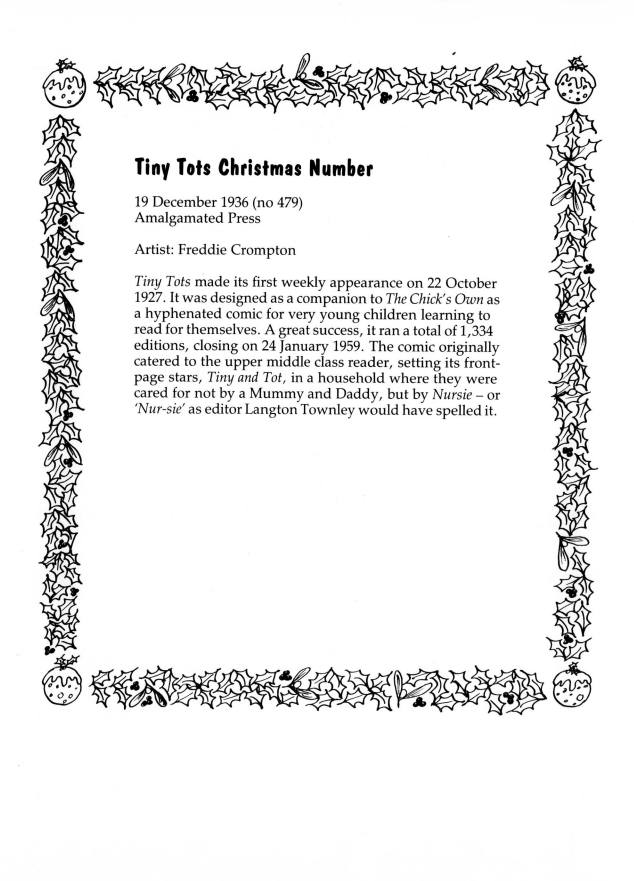

Tiny Tots Christmas Number

19 December 1936 (no 479)
Amalgamated Press

Artist: Freddie Crompton

Tiny Tots made its first weekly appearance on 22 October 1927. It was designed as a companion to *The Chick's Own* as a hyphenated comic for very young children learning to read for themselves. A great success, it ran a total of 1,334 editions, closing on 24 January 1959. The comic originally catered to the upper middle class reader, setting its front-page stars, *Tiny and Tot*, in a household where they were cared for not by a Mummy and Daddy, but by *Nursie* – or *'Nur-sie'* as editor Langton Townley would have spelled it.

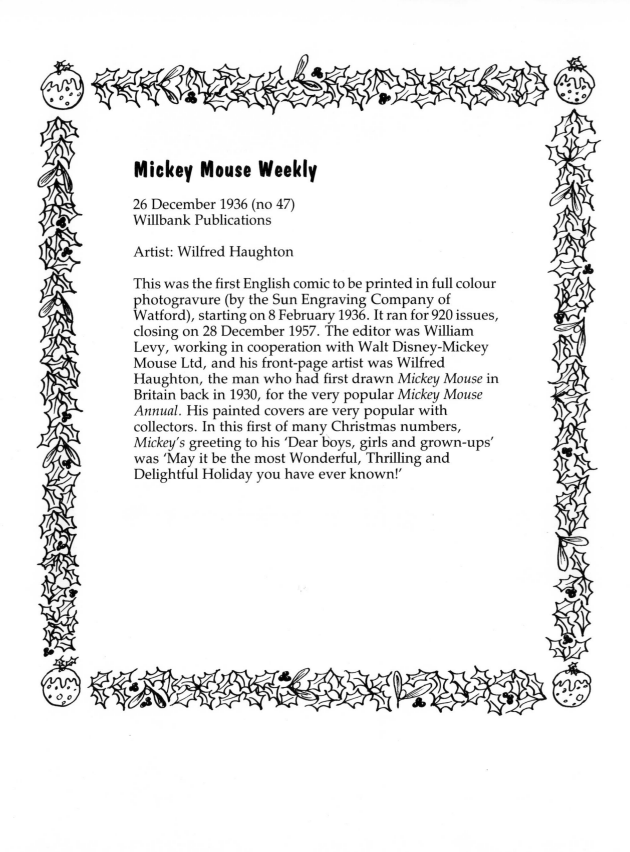

Mickey Mouse Weekly

26 December 1936 (no 47)
Willbank Publications

Artist: Wilfred Haughton

This was the first English comic to be printed in full colour photogravure (by the Sun Engraving Company of Watford), starting on 8 February 1936. It ran for 920 issues, closing on 28 December 1957. The editor was William Levy, working in cooperation with Walt Disney-Mickey Mouse Ltd, and his front-page artist was Wilfred Haughton, the man who had first drawn *Mickey Mouse* in Britain back in 1930, for the very popular *Mickey Mouse Annual*. His painted covers are very popular with collectors. In this first of many Christmas numbers, *Mickey's* greeting to his 'Dear boys, girls and grown-ups' was 'May it be the most Wonderful, Thrilling and Delightful Holiday you have ever known!'

The Joker Merry Xmas Number

2 January 1937 (no 479)
Amalgamated Press

Artist: John Jukes

The Joker had started on 5 November 1927 as an
independent comic published by the Fleetway Press.
However, after only twelve weeks it was taken over by the
mighty Amalgamated Press and became one of their best
penny comics under editor Richard Chance. The popular
front-page hero, *Alfie the Air Tramp* who flew a sort of
Flying Flea steered by *Wagger the Sky Terrier's* tail, was
created by Albert Pease, but really reached the heights
under the stylish pen of John L. Jukes. His wonderful
Christmas cover includes most of the comic's inside
characters, from *Dicky Duffer the Dunce* to *King Oolah the
Ebony Ruler*.

PUCK
MERRY CHRISTMAS NUMBER

No. 1,743.] **DON AND DORIS HAVE A JOLLY CHRISTMAS TREAT.** December 25th, 1937.

1. Dear Everybody,—Little knowing that a nasty old man was plotting to upset us, Doris and I were looking forward to spending a merry Christmas, for on the toboggan we carried a basketful of presents.

2. Yes, we were getting along quite nicely until Woodland Willie put the brake on our toboggan with his walking-stick. "Whoops! We've run over something!" I cried. "You're telling me!" said Doris.

3. Then after bouncing up into the air, our sledge took a rise out of us while that nasty old man took our basket and his departure. "Aha! All for me!" he chuckled. "Fancy these presents coming my way!"

4. But before I had a chance to look round, our toboggan bowled over a young sapling, and I thought we had struck lucky. "Look! Here's our Christmas tree, Doris!" I cried. "Where's our basket?" she said.

5. Of course, we searched high and low and in between, but we had to carry on without it in the end. But I guessed we were on the right track when a few ticks later I saw Woodland Willie in the distance.

6. Now a poor little orphan boy was standing in the gutter with a home-made Christmas tree, and he begged the old man to spare something for it. "Hee-hee! That will do for the present!" said Woodland Willie.

7. Oh dear! Wasn't the poor little fellow upset when Willie tossed him only a banana' peel! But the nasty man got upset himself, and the basket of goodies, when we gave him a lift with our Christmas tree.

8. "Hooray! Now things are looking up!" cried the orphan boy, when our pudding and presents came down on his umbrella-tree. "Ha, ha! That's very funny!" laughed Mr. Puck, who happened to be passing.

9. And our jolly old friend, the Editor, was so pleased that he invited us all to a grand Christmas party. On the way we were joined by Rinty, Tiny Tim and his pets, the Jolliboys, and all your merry old favourites.

10. I feel sure it must have been the jolliest Christmas party that ever was, for everyone had a gorgeous time, especially when Santa Claus served up the Christmas pudding. Then there was a tremendous Christmas tree loaded with presents for all, after which your jolly old friend, the Editor, raised his glass and we all drank the following toast—

Here's Wishing all Puck Readers a Happy Christmas Full of Good Things and Good Times

Puck Merry Christmas Number

25 December 1937 (no 1743)
Amalgamated Press

Artist: Roy Wilson

This colourful Christmas cover shows cartoonist Roy
Wilson at his priceless peak, toys tumbling down the sides,
a beautifully lettered title, and a double helping of heroes.
Don and *Doris*, who started their page one fun earlier in
1937, come to a Christmas climax in picture nine with
virtually all the current *Puck* stars, the boys of *Dr Jolliboy's*
school, *Rin-Tin-Tin the Wonder Dog*, and even *Mr Puck* the
editor, all crammed in, while along the bottom of the page,
Tiny Timothy throws a party for his many pets. As the
editor promised inside, 'Puck'll make you chuckle!'

GOLDEN PICTURE PALACE

No. 10.] LIEUTENANT DARING AND JOLLY ROGER, THE BOLD SEA ROVERS [DECEMBER 25th, 1937.

It's no joke catching all the snow.
But a feed soon warms Postman Joe.

1. Our jolly sea rovers were loaded with presents for their friends when they landed in good old England just in time for Christmas. The first person they saw was an old sailor selling bootlaces. "We'll help him," they said.

2. But before our two kind hearts could offer old Stumpy a handsome price for his entire stock they found themselves pushed off the pavement by a huge snowball. "Great icebergs, what a storm!" piped the parrot.

3. "Wow! I've lost all my laces! I'm ruined!" gasped the poor pedlar. But the big fellow only laughed as he pushed on with his snowball and carried all before him. "Hi, come back!" cried Roger. "About turn!"

4. But did the big fellow come back? No, not he! So our tip-top tall tar quickly threw a native club at the signboard hanging outside the village inn. "That should make him sign off his very taking ways!" cried Daring.

5. That was a very well-timed drop-shot and it made the signboard break away from its moorings and put the brake on that snowball nicely. "Oh, nice work, sir!" cried Roger, on seeing the bad lad had gone quite adrift.

6. Then up rushed our chums to try to find the old pedlar's stock-in-trade. "Don't worry, old-timer, here's your laces!" said Daring. But when they pulled them out of that large snowball—oh, what a surprise!

7. Yes, that artful lad had used the snowball to try to get some scent and cigars past the Excise officers. "You can leave Smuggler Sam to us!" they said. "You're welcome to the handsome reward for his capture!"

8. "Thanks muchly!" said the gallant lieutenant. "Now we can all drop in at the Dewdrop Inn and give the old pedlar a Christmas feed!" They had a jolly time, and I hope all GOLDEN readers have the same.

Golden

25 December 1937 (no 10)
Amalgamated Press

Artist: Roy Wilson

Golden Fun and Story was a comic in the tradition of *Tip Top* and *Jingles,* a two-colour comic for one penny. It started on 23 October 1937, and this is its first Happy Christmas number. Roy Wilson went to town as usual on his double-feature cover, reviving *Lieutenant Daring and Jolly Roger, the Bold Sea Rovers* from *Sparkler,* and adding a downward series of one-off strips under the title of *The Golden Picture Palace.* The genial chap in the top left-hand corner of the title is the editor, *Sam Smiles.* Inside he asks, 'Why is my name the longest name in the world?' Easy – 'because there's a mile between the first and last letter!' He adds, 'I love Christmas. I've just had my chimney swept in case Father Christmas thinks I'm not too much of an old boy to call on!'

FUNNY WONDER 2d
CHRISTMAS DOUBLE NUMBER

No. 1239   Pitch, Toss, and Occy Perform a Neat Feat with Socks.   Dec. 25th, 1937.

1. It looked as if Daddy Christmas would have to work overtime when Pitch, Toss, Pengy, and Occy hung up their socks. "Greedy lot," said Captain Codseye.

2. Our merry mariners bunked into their bunks and the skipper prepared to stock their socks. "I'll have a lark and give them their presents later," he cooed.

3. Pengy nearly gave the game away when he helped himself to a beakful of beard. "Hoi!" the skipper gasped. "Leave the old chin upholstery alone!"

4. Pitch and Toss were pretending to sleep each with one eye shut and the other eye closed, and so didn't see the skipper parking big knobs of coal in their socks.

5. A few half ticks later the captain toddled out and our saucy salts made a dive for their socks. But Occy was before them, feeling with his feelers for his presents.

6. Meanwhile, Codseye had met a spot of bother in the shape of two toughs who politely told him to turn out his pockets quick before he got a faceful of black eyes.

7. "Ah! Something like a Christmas present," grinned one large laddie. "It's more blessed to give than receive, so you blessed-well give all you've got!"

8. Now, in their cabin, Pitch and Toss were putting Occy in his place. "Hoi! Unhook your greedy graspers!" said Pitch. "Sailors before octopussies," cried Toss.

9. Occy did as bid, the socks flew back and out through the porthole whizzed their cargoes of coal. "Coo! Do you see what I see, chum?" said Pitch.

10. By a spot of luck the toughs got in the way of that fuel and went out quicker than fires in a flood. "Ah! A 'coaled' reception," said Codseye wittily.

11. Pitch, Toss, Pengy, and Occy trooped out to see what was which and the skipper made whoopes with them. "A jolly good Christmas 'heave,'" he gurgled.

12. So our pals got their Christmas presents and invitations to munch with the skipper and his nieces and, filling their pop glasses, wish you a Merry Christmas.

Funny Wonder Christmas Double Number

25 December 1937 (no 1239)
Amalgamated Press

Artist: Roy Wilson

Yes, that is Charlie Chaplin in the top left-hand corner of the title cartoon. He was once the famous front page star of *Funny Wonder*, but by this Christmas number was to be found on the inside. Roy Wilson's third Christmas cover of the season starred his regular merry mariners, *Pitch and Toss*, with their seafaring pets, *Pengy the Penguin* and *Occy the Octopus*, not forgetting, of course, good old *Captain Codseye*. *Funny Wonder* was one of the longest running of Alfred Harmsworth's comics, starting on 4 February 1893 and ending, as *Wonder*, on 12 September 1953, a sixty-year span. This double number enclosed no fewer than three free gifts, all for twopence.

Playbox

24 December 1938 (no 723)
Amalgamated Press

Artist: Freddie Crompton

Playbox has one of the longest histories of any British comic, starting as a weekly pull-out supplement to Harmsworth's *Home Chat*, a woman's magazine, on 29 October 1898, edited by Leicester Harmsworth under the name of *Aunt Molly*. It became a coloured monthly comic supplement to the magazine *The World and his Wife* from November 1904, and also ran as a supplement to the juvenile magazine, *The New Children's Encyclopaedia* from May 1910. It became a proper comic on 14 February 1925, but with a difference. It was the first comic for girls. Not a success, it widened its appeal and eventually clocked up 1,279 issues, ending on 11 June 1955. Here the front page features *Sonny Bear and Micky*, who ran from 1935 to the end.

Happy Days

31 December 1938 (no 13)
Amalgamated Press

Artist: Roy Wilson

Of all the many Christmas comic covers drawn by genius Roy Wilson, this has to be the best. *Happy Days* was the first Amalgamated Press comic to be printed in full colour photogravure, answering the challenge of *Mickey Mouse Weekly*. Wilson's work was so terrific that the Editor, John Bott, allowed him to sign it every week. Wilson's rare all-animal strip, *Happy Days at Chimpo's Circus*, starred *Chimpo the clown*, *Jum the elephant*, *Crackle the pig*, and *Lordy Leo the ring-master lion*. Alas, they did not prove strong enough rivals for *Mickey Mouse* and his chums, and *Happy Days* wound up after only 45 issues.

RADIO FUN 2D

No. 11,
Dec. 24th,
1938.
EVERY THURSDAY

"GEORGE, THE JOLLY GEE-GEE"

Radio Fun

24 December 1938 (no 11)
Amalgamated Press

Artist: Roy Wilson

Radio Fun started on 15 October 1938, marking the Golden Age of the wireless set. Its twenty-eight pages for twopence featured such stars as Arthur Askey (Big-hearted Arthur) from *Band Wagon,* Sandy Powell (Can you hear me, Mother?), Bud Flanagan and Chesney Allen (Oi!), Ethel Revnell and Gracie West (the long and short of it), backed up by film stars Tom Keene and Clark Gable. The cover was one of Roy Wilson's best creations, *George the Jolly Gee-Gee,* but having no connection with radio, he soon disappeared inside. The page was drawn without speech balloons as a 'silent' strip, but Jack Pamby added them on editor Stanley Gooch's orders.

Bumper Christmas Number

THE DANDY COMIC

No 159 · DEC 14TH 1940
EVERY FRIDAY
2D

KORKY the CAT

SEE KORKY SAVE THESE KIDS A ROW.
THEIR SNOWMAN'S LIKE OLD NASTY NOW.
AND THEN HE WRITES UPON THE WALL
HIS GREETINGS TO YOU ONE AND ALL.

The Dandy Comic Bumper Christmas Number

14 December 1940 (no 159)
D. C. Thomson

Artist: James Crichton

The Dandy Comic came suddenly from Dundee on 4 December 1937, blowing a fresh style into the traditions of Alfred Harmsworth's Amalgamated Press. It was a smaller size than the standard tabloid, and presented twenty-eight pages for twopence, each one packed with laughs or thrills. *Korky the Cat* is still running today, despite the demise of his original artist, and of course, *Desperate Dan* remains, tough as ever, over now on page one.

This wartime Christmas issue also featured a strip series starring *Addie and Hermy the Nasty Nazis*.

The Beano Xmas Comic

14 December 1940 (no 125)
D. C. Thomson

Artist: Reg Carter

The Beano Comic was the swift follow-through to *Dandy*, sending the Amalgamated Press into a panic. Twenty-eight pages for twopence, it was as big a bargain as its companion, and closely modelled on the winning formula devised by R. D. Low and Albert Barnes, editors. Reg Carter was an old-timer in comics, having started with comic postcards early in the century. His *Big Eggo* the ostrich reigned on the cover from number 1 (30 July 1938), but was replaced some years later by *Biffo the Bear*, drawn by the top Thomson artist, Dudley D Watkins.

THE **MAGIC** COMIC

Nº 74 · DEC 14ᵀᴴ 1940
EVERY THURSDAY
2ᴰ

KOKO the PUP

ON CHRISTMAS EVE, CUTE KOKO, THE WRETCH
HANGS UP A STOCKING THAT WILL STRETCH.
BUT NOW OUR PUP DON'T FEEL SO PLEASANT
'COS HE AIN'T GOT A SINGLE PRESENT!

The Magic Comic Bumper Christmas Number

14 December 1940 (no 74)
D. C. Thomson

Artist: James Crichton

The third Christmas comic published the same week of 1940 by D. C. Thomson of Dundee, was that of *The Magic Comic*. This weekly started on 22 July 1939, again modelled on the successful *Dandy-Beano* formula, but this time aimed at a younger audience. *Koko the Pup,* the front-page animal hero, was created by Harry Banger, but here James Crichton of *Korky the Cat* fame has taken over for Christmas. *Magic* had fewer pages than its two companions, but as an extra treat offered an entire spread and back page in full colours, which looked just fine on *The Tickler Twins in Wonderland* and *Hiram Scaram the Stage-coach Driver*. *Magic* folded after eighty issues.

Here's A Happy Christmas to Every Girl and Boy! **2D**

KNOCK-OUT
COMIC AND "MAGNET"

No. 96.
December 28th, 1940.

EVERY WEDNESDAY.

Knockout Comic and Magnet

28 December 1940 (no 96)
Amalgamated Press

Artist: Hugh McNeill

The Knock-Out Comic was the Amalgamated Press's answer to D. C. Thomson's *Dandy* and *Beano,* and a brilliant one. Not only did it imitate their format of twenty-eight pages for twopence, it featured a host of old favourites alongside the new comic characters. *Sexton Blake,* the daring detective of story-papers since 1898, appeared in an exciting picture serial, and *Billy Bunter,* famous fat boy of the Greyfriars Remove, was also a comic strip star. Bunter's weekly, *The Magnet,* was discontinued due to the wartime paper shortage, and was incorporated with *Knock-Out.* But the comic's real star was cartoonist Hugh McNeill, whose rollicking style was not only to be seen on the front pages, but inside with such strips as *Our Ernie, Simon the Simple Sleuth,* and *Our Happy Vakkies,* about wartime evacuees. *Knock-Out* ran 1,251 issues, ending on 16 February 1963.

Everyday Novels and Comics 2d

THE XMAS EXPLOITS OF BILLY AND BRENDA BROWN, THE SUNSHINE TWINS OF LONDON TOWN.

Our Sunshine Twins stopped as they saw their dad, Pa Brown, doing a posh bit of bill-posting. "Coo! It's a cold Christmas!" bleated Billy. "Yes, and we're broke," Brenda told her brother. Y'see, someone had broken in and stolen all the kids' carol-singing money from the mantel-shelf. That's why they were interested in that "Wanted" notice their dad was pasting up.

"Look, Sis, a reward offered for that roughneck!" Billy hissed. "Yes, and Soapy Sam's the sneak who pinched our pennies," said his sister. They knew because he'd left the marks of his dirty hands on the mantel-shelf. Soapy Sam never washed—hence his name. There was £5 reward for his arrest. "Coo! Could we use that coin?" cried Billy.

So our kids got cracking. It was tough G-man stuff, looking for Soapy Sam. But right off they spotted a suspicious bloke who seemed to be choking himself in his hankie. "Suspicious the way he sneezes," hissed our hero. To our kids it looked like Soapy Sam trying to disguise his handsome features.

Our kids hung closer to that bloke than his shadow, till the guy began to get uncomfortable like. He dropped the wiper and whipped around. "Sheer off! Think this is a pantomime, and I'm the clown?" he snoozed. "Atishoo! Oh, what a cold!" he wailed. "It's a poor look-out if a bloke can't blow his conk without collecting a crowd."

Well, it wasn't Soapy Sam. They saw that. And they sheered off, a bit discouraged. After wandering round the streets and underneath the arches for another three hours, things began to look really bleak. "Soapy Sam's somewhere in this city," insisted Sis. "Well, you can search me," said her brother. "But what you said about going home goes for me too. I quit."

Like sensible kids, they agreed to go home and get their tea. And they were toddling along when they suddenly saw Santa Claus standing with a sack full of lucky dips. "It's one penny per person per paw put in. What say? I'll race you for a penn'orth," proposed Billy. Next moment they were running to see who should have a lucky dip first.

Of course, little brother Billy began to beat his sister. He shot ahead, but just as he was winning the race he lost control of his legs. Most awkward, of course, in the snow, and as he looked like falling on his face Billy made a grab at the nearest thing—which happened to be Santa Claus' snowy beard. And was that man mortified? "Here, leggo!" he howled.

Bill was sorry—but he couldn't oblige. He hung on to the hairy ornament like glue. And he pulled Father Christmas down with somewhat of a nasty smack ere the glue on the beard came unstuck. Biff! Crack! Even his hat came off. And the twins stared at the nasty features of the man who had pinched their money-box as well as various other valuables.

Yes, it was Soapy Sam, the dirty old man. Y'see, he'd planned to crack many cribs in that part of the neighbourhood over Christmas, and he'd hit on the plan of disguising himself to dodge the police. But he couldn't fool our kids, could he? Sis went off and fetched her father, who parted up with the £5 reward on the spot. And did they make whoopee? Boy!

Everyday Novels and Comics

December 1940
Popular Fiction

Artist: Jack Greenall

Cartoonist Jack Greenall was never too lucky with his comic work. He had contributed cartoon jokes and illustrations to *The Boy's Magazine* in the Twenties, and later several strips to *The Jolly Comic* and *Sparkler*, without great success. He struck lucky with the *Daily Mirror*, however, and his regular joke about *Useless Eustace* was a popular favourite for many years. This rare comic, a one-shot, was put out under the wartime restrictions which prevented new regular publications. The publisher, Popular Fiction, also issued a pocket-sized children's story-paper entitled *Modern Fairy Tales,* which was also illustrated by Greenall.

CHIPS GRAND XMAS NUMBER 2ᴰ

No. 2,669.

The Festive Frolics of Weary Willie and Tired Tim.

December 27th, 1941.

1. Dear Festive Ones,—'Twas Christmastide, and Willie and Tim were doing a bit of carol warbling in the hope of collecting some funds for the festivities. They made a start outside the homestead of a certain Mr. Gregory Grump.

2. Now, Gregory Grump was a mingy old frump, and the concert outside gave him the hump. So he opened the windows with a couple of jerks, and gave our melody lads the works. A terrible blow was that dose of snow.

3. Well, having dug themselves out of the snowdrift, they had a view of the inside of old Grump's villa, and there was the frowsy old frostbite gloating over his Christmas fare. And the sight gave Willie an idea for a real fare share-out.

4. So having sent Tim round to the other window, he unpocketed a bob and dropped it on the floor. "Look out, mister, you've dropped a bob!" he chanted. "You mustn't start throwing your money about in these hard times."

5. Well, greedy old Grump didn't lose any time in pouncing on that boblet, and as he did a quick bend, he biffed the table with his sit-down and sent it across the room to where Tim was waiting to receive anything that came his way.

6. And then the tubby larker did a bit of rapid wrapping up. "This is just what the doctor ordered," he twittered. "I always believe in taking a good meal when you're peckish; and this lot is cheap at the price of a bob."

7. There wasn't any need to trouble old Grump with their presence after that, so they ambled merrily on their way. "That bob of yours couldn't have done us a better turn if it had been Bob Tanner's lucky sixpence," tooted Tim.

8. In due time home was reached, and they set out the spread. "We'll get on with this straight away and make no bones about it," whiffled Willie. Now, at this moment old Grump was peering in through the window and plotting a plot.

9. "Aha, they shall not diddle me out of my grub," he croaked, and with a crafty chuckle he lowered himself down the coalhole. Now, you may think that he had decided to go and eat coke—certainly not. He had planned a plan.

10. Now, Gregory Grump had spotted that the grub laden table was standing on a trapdoor, and he worked it out that if he opened the trap the feast would come down his way.

11. But as they were using the tablecloth ends as bibs, only the table vanished. "Summat's happened," fluted Tim, "but the grub is still on the menu. Let the party proceed."

12. It did and all, and our merry pals send you all hearty greetings folks, and hope that you will have a tasty time, too. More larks in a fortnight's time, Chipites.—CORNY CHIPS.

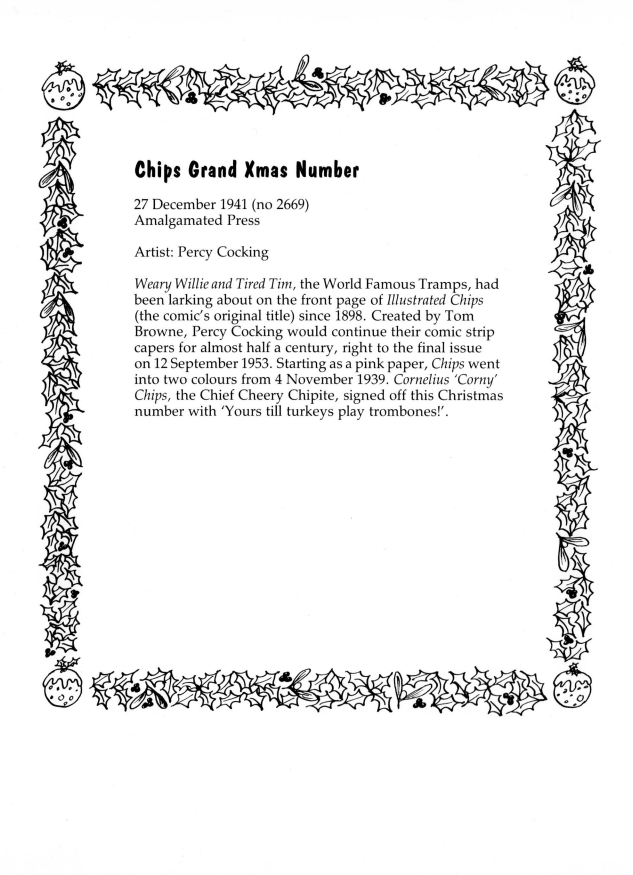

Chips Grand Xmas Number

27 December 1941 (no 2669)
Amalgamated Press

Artist: Percy Cocking

Weary Willie and Tired Tim, the World Famous Tramps, had been larking about on the front page of *Illustrated Chips* (the comic's original title) since 1898. Created by Tom Browne, Percy Cocking would continue their comic strip capers for almost half a century, right to the final issue on 12 September 1953. Starting as a pink paper, *Chips* went into two colours from 4 November 1939. *Cornelius 'Corny' Chips,* the Chief Cheery Chipite, signed off this Christmas number with 'Yours till turkeys play trombones!'.